DIABETIC CO
FOR BEGIN

1200 Days of Easy & Tasty Diabetic Recipes with a 30 Days Meal Plan to Lower Your Blood Sugar and Help you Manage Prediabetes

Poula Ray

Table of Contents

- # Introduction

Diabetic recipes can help you keep blood sugar levels in control without compromising taste and flavor. They are suitable for parties and can be made part of your regular eating habits. There are plenty of recipes on the internet that are suitable for diabetics. You can also consult a nutritionist if you are unsure about a particular recipe.

Diabetics must also watch portion sizes and balance their diet. They must make sure they get the same amount of carbohydrates in each meal. To help you stick to this, there are four tips to follow. First of all, always check your blood sugar level. Second, stick to a set number of carbohydrates per meal, which is usually 45 to 75 grams.

One of the easiest diabetic dinners is stir-fries. These delicious and healthy dishes are packed with vegetables. As a lean protein, chicken is a great choice. The American Diabetes Association suggests choosing chicken without the skin, as this reduces the amount of saturated fat and cholesterol. A few other ingredients, like garlic, jalapeno, fresh ginger, and lime, add flavor. You can also use reduced soy sauce instead of salt. A lot of salt can raise blood pressure and increase your risk of heart disease.

Information about diabetes

Whether you've been diagnosed with diabetes or are looking for tips to manage your condition, the information in the diabetic cookbook can help you make informed decisions. It contains recipes and nutrition information, as well as meal plans and self-compassion techniques to help you manage your disease. It can even help you avoid the pitfalls of diabetes by teaching you to eat healthy and reduce your insulin production.

If you're newly diagnosed with Type 2 diabetes, you will likely need to change your diet and nutrition habits. The information in the diabetic cookbook will help you make these changes without feeling deprived.

Most diabetic cookbooks focus on meal replacement and building a better diet. Diabetics need to be extra careful about their meals. They must also pay attention to the sugar and carb content of their meals. Diabetic cookbooks should provide easy-to-follow meal planning instructions. However, be sure to consult with your doctor to develop a specific plan for you.

Chapter 1: The Benefits of the Diabetes Meal Prep

Meal prepping is an excellent way to control diabetes. Not only does it make it easier to choose foods rich in healthy fats, but it can also help you lose weight. Many people with type 2 diabetes are overweight or obese. By preparing meals ahead of time, you can save yourself money and time, and still enjoy delicious meals.

Clean eating recipes of diabetic meal planning

For those who are already diabetic or are at risk for developing the disease, meal planning can be a valuable tool. Not only will it help you stay on track with your blood glucose levels, but it can also help you maintain a healthy weight. In addition, a clean diet can help you avoid the complications associated with diabetes, such as high blood pressure.

It is vital to plan your meals ahead of time and prepare them accordingly. Many people are busy and don't have time to prepare nutritious meals. A meal plan can help you keep track of the calories and carbohydrates that you eat throughout the day. It also helps make healthy eating more enjoyable. However, a diet that is too restrictive can make it hard for you to meet your nutritional needs. With meal planning, you can create tasty meals that are easy to prepare.

The key to achieving blood glucose control with clean eating recipes for diabetics is to balance your carbohydrates. You should aim for 45-60 grams of carbohydrates per meal. This amount may vary depending on your diet and lifestyle. Your doctor or a registered dietitian can help you determine the best percentage of carbohydrates in your diet.

Benefits of diabetic meal planning

Diabetic meal planning is an excellent tool to use in managing diabetes. This type of planning can help you choose healthier ingredients, and it can also help you reduce the amount of sugar you eat. In addition to helping you maintain a healthy blood glucose level, meal planning can also help you lose weight. Many people with diabetes are overweight or obese.

Diabetics should plan their meals so that they include foods high in fiber. This will help them keep a healthy weight, and will help them hit their target blood glucose levels. This will lead to fewer diabetes complications. This will help them live longer and feel better. However, meal planning is not always as easy as it seems.

It also helps to control portion size, so that you don't overeat or undereat. You can also use meal prep to make your meals more appealing. For instance, you can make chicken breast with pesto sauce and pair it with whole wheat spaghetti and sliced carrots. Both of these foods are rich in healthy fats.

People with diabetes should make sure that they are eating three times a day. They need to avoid sugar spikes and keep their blood sugar levels in a consistent range. They should also be conscious of how much carbohydrates they consume in each meal. Too much or too little carbohydrates can spike blood sugar levels, which is not good for those with diabetes.

People with diabetes must take their medications on time and regularly, monitor blood glucose levels, and learn to eat a healthy diet. This can be challenging to do. Meal prep helps them achieve these goals by saving time, energy, and money. It is also a great way to establish a healthy routine.

Meal prep helps people with diabetes plan out their meals ahead of time. They can use meal prep to learn which foods they like and which ones they should avoid. This can also help them learn which foods are best for them and how to incorporate them into their diet. Meal prep can also reduce stress and temptations around cooking and shopping.

Chapter 2: Breakfast Recipes

Recipe 1: Almond Nuggets

Serving Size: 4

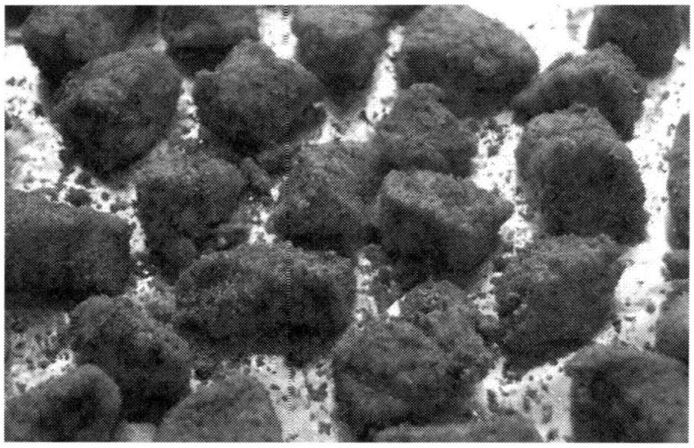

Cooking Time: 23 minutes

Ingredients:

- 1 egg white
- 1 tablespoon freshly squeezed lemon juice
- ½ teaspoon dried basil
- ½ teaspoon ground paprika
- 1 lb low-sodium boneless, skinless chicken breasts, 1 ½-inch cubes
- ½ cup ground almonds
- 2 slices low-sodium whole-wheat bread, crumbled

Directions:

1. With a fork, whisk together the egg white, lemon juice, basil, and paprika in a small basin until frothy. Add the chicken and stir to coat.
2. On a plate, mix the almonds and bread crumbs. Toss the chicken cubes in the almond and bread crumb mixture until coated.
3. Bake the nuggets in the air fryer, in two batches, at 400°F (204°C) for 10 to 13 minutes, or until the chicken reaches an internal temperature of 165°F (74°C) on a meat thermometer. Serve immediately.

Nutritional Value: Calories 275; Fat 4.2g; Carbohydrates 5g; Protein 32g

Recipe 2: Artichoke Frittata

Serving Size: 4

Cooking Time: 10 minutes

Ingredients:

- 8 large eggs
- ¼ cup Asiago cheese, grated
- 1 tablespoon fresh basil, chopped
- 1 teaspoon fresh oregano, chopped
- Pinch of salt
- 1 teaspoon extra virgin olive oil
- 1 teaspoon garlic, minced
- 1 cup canned artichokes, drained
- 1 tomato, chopped

Directions:

1. Pre-heat your oven to broil. Take a medium bowl and whisk eggs, Asiago cheese, oregano, basil, sea salt, and pepper. Blend in a bowl.
2. In a large ovenproof skillet, heat the olive oil. Sauté for 1 minute after adding the garlic. Take the skillet from the heat and add the egg mixture.
3. Return skillet to heat and sprinkle artichoke hearts and tomato over eggs. Cook frittata without stirring for 8 minutes.
4. Broil skillet for 1 minute until lightly browned. Cut frittata into 4 pieces and serve. Enjoy!

Nutritional Value: Calories 199; Fat 13g; Carbohydrates 5g; Protein 16g

Recipe 3: Avocado and Bacon Rolls

Serving Size: 2

Cooking Time: 25 minutes

Ingredients:

- 2 avocados
- ½ lime
- 250 grams of bacon
- 1 tablespoon olive oil
- sea-salt
- pepper

Directions:

1. Halve and core the avocados
2. Quarter the avocados, remove the pulp from the skin, and drizzle with lime juice.
3. Spread the slices of bacon on a board and roll up the avocado pieces one after the other.
4. Heat the oil in the pan and fry the avocados with the bacon on all sides.
5. Season everything with salt and pepper.

Nutritional Value: Calories 135; Fat 6.6g; Carbohydrates 34g; Protein 26.6g

Recipe 4: Avocado Goat Cheese Toast

Serving Size: 2

Cooking Time: 10 minutes

Ingredients:

- 2 slices whole-wheat thin-sliced bread
- ½ avocado
- 2 tablespoons crumbled goat cheese
- Salt, to taste

Directions:

1. In a toaster or broiler, toast the bread until browned.
2. Remove the flesh from the avocado. In a medium bowl, use a regular-sized fork to mash the avocado flesh. Spread it onto the toast.
3. Sprinkle with the goat cheese and season lightly with salt.
4. Add any toppings and serve.

Nutritional Value: Calories 137; Fat 6g; Carbohydrates 18g; Protein 5g

Recipe 5: Bacon and Brie Omelet Wedges

Serving Size: 6

Cooking Time: 10 minutes

Ingredients:

- 2 tablespoons olive oil
- 7 ounces smoked bacon
- 6 beaten eggs
- Small bunch chives, snipped
- 3 ½ ounces brie, sliced
- 1 teaspoon red wine vinegar
- 1 teaspoon Dijon mustard
- 1 cucumber, halved, deseeded, and sliced diagonally
- 7 ounces radish, quartered

Directions:

1. Dissolve In a large saucepan over medium heat, melt 2 tablespoons of butter. Mix in the thyme and halibut and cook
2. Uncover and put it back into the oven for another 20 minutes until it's bubbling. Let it rest for 15 minutes. You can sprinkle it with some parsley before serving.

Nutritional Value: Calories 343; Fat 15.4g; Carbohydrates 39.4g; Protein 13.8g

Recipe 6: Bacon Jalapeno Wraps

Serving Size: 4

Cooking Time: 10 minutes

Ingredients:

- 1 package bacon, uncured and nitrate free
- 6 fresh jalapeno peppers, halved lengthwise and seeded
- 1 (8 ounce) package cream cheese
- 1 dozen toothpicks, soaked

Directions:

1. Preheat your griddle to high heat.
2. Fill jalapeno halves with cream cheese.
3. Wrap each with bacon. Secure with a toothpick.
4. Place on the prepared griddle, and cook until bacon is crispy, about 5 to 7 minutes per side.
5. Remove to a medium-sized platter to cool and serve warm.

Nutritional Value: Calories 279; Fat 33.4g; Carbohydrates 3.5g; Protein 16.3g

Recipe 7: Bang Bang Cauliflower

Serving Size: 4

Cooking Time: 35 minutes

Ingredients:

- 1 large cauliflower
- 3 tablespoon of olive oil
- 2 tablespoon of sweet chili sauce
- 1 tablespoon of Sriracha sauce
- 2 tablespoon of lime juice
- 3 cloves of garlic (diced)
- Kosher salt
- Black pepper powder
- 1 tablespoon of cilantro (chopped)

Directions:

1. Preheat the oven - 425°F.
2. Separate all the florets of cauliflower.
3. Take a bowl, add sweet chili sauce, Sriracha sauce, garlic, olive oil, and lime juice. Mix well.
4. Add the cauliflower florets into the bowl of sauce. Toss it until the florets absorb the sauce entirely.
5. Keep it on a baking sheet and season it with black pepper powder and salt.
6. Keep in the oven and roast for 35 minutes.
7. Take out and serve after garnishing with cilantro.

Nutritional Value: Calories 199; Fat 13g; Carbohydrates 5g; Protein 16g

Recipe 8: Beef and Broccoli

Serving Size: 2

Cooking Time: 10 minutes

Ingredients:

- 6 stripped beef roast slices
- 1 chopped scallion
- 3 oz chopped broccoli florets
- 1 tablespoon avocado oil
- 1 tablespoon unsalted butter

Seasoning:

- ¼ teaspoon salt
- 1/8 teaspoon ground black pepper
- 1 ½ tablespoon soy sauce
- 3 tablespoon chicken broth

Directions:

1. Take a medium skillet pan, place it over medium heat, add the oil and when hot, add the beef strips and cook for 2 minutes until hot.
2. Transfer the beef to a plate, add the scallion to the pan, add the butter, and cook for 3 minutes until tender.
3. Add the remaining ingredients, stir until mixed, switch heat to the low level, and simmer for 3 to 4 minutes until the broccoli is tender.
4. Return the beef to the pan, stir until well combined, and cook for 1 minute.

Nutritional Value: Calories 265; Fat 9g; Carbohydrates 16g; Protein 19.6g

Recipe 9: Breakfast Taco Scramble

Serving Size: 4

Cooking Time: 1 hour and 25 minutes

Ingredients:

- 8 large eggs, beaten
- 1/4 teaspoon seasoning salt
- 1 lb. 99% lean ground turkey
- 2 tablespoon Greek seasoning
- 1/2 small onion, minced
- 2 tablespoons of bell pepper, minced
- 4 ounces can tomato sauce
- 1/4 cup of water
- 1/4 cup of chopped scallions or cilantro for topping

For the potatoes:

- 12 baby gold or red potatoes, quartered
- 4 teaspoon of olive oil
- 3/4 teaspoon of salt
- 1/2 teaspoon of garlic powder
- fresh black pepper, to taste

Directions:

1. Beat the eggs in a large mixing basin with seasoning salt. Preheat the oven to 425 degrees F. Spray a 9x12 or large oval casserole dish with cooking oil. Add the potatoes 1 tablespoon oil, 3/4 teaspoon salt, garlic powder, and black pepper and toss to coat. Bake for 45 minutes to an hour, stirring 15 minutes in between.
2. In the meantime, brown the turkey in a large skillet over medium heat, breaking it up while it cooks. Once no longer pink, add in the Greek seasoning. Add bell pepper, onion, tomato sauce, and water, stir and cover, simmer on low for about 20 minutes. Spray a different skillet with nonstick spray over medium heat.
3. Once heated, add in the eggs seasoned with 1/4 teaspoon of salt and scramble for 2–3 minutes, or cook until it sets. Distribute 3/4 cup turkey and 2/3 cup eggs, divide the potatoes in each storage container, and store for 3-4 days.

Nutritional Value: Calories 215; Fat 6.6g; Carbohydrates 14g; Protein 26.6g

Recipe 10: Cabbage and Coconut Chia Smoothie

Serving Size: 2

Cooking Time: 5 minutes

Ingredients:

- 1/3 cup cabbage
- 1 cup cold unsweetened coconut milk
- 1 tablespoon chia seeds
- ½ cup cherries
- ½ cup spinach

Directions:

1. Add coconut milk to your blender
2. Cut cabbage and add to your blender
3. Place chia seeds in a coffee grinder and chop to powder; brush the powder into your blender
4. Pit the cherries and add them to your blender
5. Wash and dry the spinach and chop
6. Add to the mix
7. Cover and blend on low followed by medium
8. Taste the texture and serve chilled!

Nutritional Value: Calories 199; Fat 13g; Carbohydrates 5g; Protein 16g

Recipe 11: Cauliflower Sausage Feast

Serving Size: 4

Cooking Time: 20 minutes

Ingredients:

- 2 cloves garlic, minced
- ½ pound turkey sausage
- 4 teaspoons olive oil (divided)
- 1 small onion, diced
- 1 pound cauliflower rice (about 4 cups)
- ⅛ teaspoon pepper
- ¼ teaspoon salt
- 3 tablespoons water
- 8 large eggs

Directions:

1. Heat 2 teaspoons of the prepared olive oil over medium heat in a medium saucepan or skillet.
2. Add the onion and garlic and stir-cook until softened and fragrant.
3. Add the sausage; stir-cook for 4–5 minutes until cooked well. Set aside.
4. Add the cauliflower rice and stir cook for 2–3 minutes until golden brown.
5. Add the salt, pepper, and water; stir-cook for 3–4 minutes until golden and tender.
6. Mix in the sausage mixture and cook for 2 minutes. Divide onto plates.
7. Heat 1 teaspoon of the olive oil over medium heat in another skillet.
8. Crack 4 eggs and cook for 2–3 minutes until the whites are well set.
9. Repeat with the remaining eggs.
10. Divide the cooked eggs equally over the sausage mixture and serve warm.

Nutritional Value: Calories 317; Fat 19g; Carbohydrates 8g; Protein 26g

Recipe 12: Chicken Wild Rice Soup

Serving Size: 6

Cooking Time: 15 minutes

Ingredients:

- 2/3 cup wild rice, uncooked
- 1 tablespoon onion, chopped finely
- 1 tablespoon fresh parsley, chopped
- 1 cup carrots, chopped
- 8-ounces chicken breast, cooked
- 2 tablespoon butter
- 1/4 cup all-purpose white flour
- 5 cups low-sodium chicken broth
- 1 tablespoon slivered almonds

Directions:

1. Start by adding rice and 2 cups broth along with ½ cup water to a cooking pot. Cook the chicken until the rice is "Al dente" and set it aside.
2. Add butter to a saucepan and melt it.
3. Stir in onion and sauté until soft, then add the flour and the remaining broth.
4. Stir it and then cook for it 1 minute; add the chicken, cooked rice, and carrots.
5. Cook for 5 minutes on simmer.
6. Garnish with almonds.
7. Serve fresh.

Nutritional Value: Calories 287; Fat 35g; Carbohydrates 21.7g; Protein 21g

Recipe 13: Couscous and Chickpeas Bowls

Serving Size: 4

Cooking Time: 6 minutes

Ingredients:

- ¾ cup whole wheat couscous
- 1 yellow onion, chopped
- 1 tablespoon olive oil
- 1 cup water
- 2 garlic cloves, minced
- 15 ounces canned chickpeas, drained and rinsed
- A pinch of salt and black pepper
- 15 ounces canned tomatoes, chopped
- 14 ounces canned artichokes, drained and chopped
- ½ cup Greek olives, pitted and chopped
- ½ teaspoon oregano, dried
- 1 tablespoon lemon juice

Directions:

1. Put the water in a pot, bring to a boil over medium heat, add the couscous, stir, take off the heat, cover the pan, leave aside for 10 minutes, and fluff with a fork.
2. In a medium-high-heat pan, heat the oil, then add the onion and cook for 2 minutes.
3. Add the other ingredients and boil for 4 minutes.
4. Add the couscous, toss, divide into bowls and serve for breakfast.

Nutritional Value: Calories 340; Fat 10g; Carbohydrates 51g; Protein 11g

Recipe 14: Crepe Cakes

Serving Size: 4

Cooking Time: 20 minutes

Ingredients:

- 4 ounces (113 g) reduced-fat plain cream cheese, softened
- 2 medium bananas
- 4 large eggs
- ½ teaspoon vanilla extract
- ⅛ teaspoon salt

Directions:

1. Heat a large skillet over low heat. Coat the cooking surface with cooking spray, and allow the pan to heat for another 2 to 3 minutes.
2. Meanwhile, in a medium bowl, mash the cream cheese and bananas together with a fork until combined. The bananas can be a little chunky.
3. Add the prepared eggs, vanilla, and salt, and mix well.
4. For each piece of cake, drop 2 tablespoons of the batter onto the warmed skillet and use the bottom of a large spoon or ladle to spread it thin. Let it cook for 7 to 9 minutes.
5. Flip the cake over and cook briefly, about 1 minute.

Nutritional Value: Calories 175; Fat 9g; Carbohydrates 15g; Protein 9g

Recipe 15: Eggs Benedict

Serving Size: 2

Cooking Time: 15 minutes

Ingredients:

- 2 eggs
- 2 slices bacon
- 1 tablespoon white wine vinegar

Hollandaise Sauce

- 1 egg yolk
- 1 teaspoon lemon juice
- 3 tablespoon salted butter, melted
- ¼ teaspoon cayenne pepper
- Black pepper
- Salt to taste

Directions:

1. Add egg yolk and lemon juice to a large, heatproof bowl and whisk to combine. Place bowl over a saucepan of boiling water to create a bain-marie and continue to whisk the egg yolk and lemon juice for 3 minutes.
2. Take the mixture off the heat and slowly pour the melted butter into the bowl, continuing to whisk.
3. Season with cayenne pepper and black pepper.
4. While the sauce is cooling, poach your eggs in a large, deep-filled saucepan of boiling water and vinegar by cracking each egg into the water separately.
5. Using a large frying pan, add some olive oil and fry your slices of bacon.
6. Serve the eggs and bacon on a large plate and pour the sauce over the food before serving hot.

Nutritional Value: Calories 198; Fat 11g; Carbohydrates 16.5g; Protein 20.5g

Recipe 16: Egg Drop Soup

Serving Size: 2

Cooking Time: 25 minutes

Ingredients:

- 2 tablespoons scallions, sliced
- A pinch of red pepper flakes
- 4 cups bone broth or 2 large bouillon cubes plus 4 cups of water
- Freshly ground pepper and salt to taste
- 2 eggs, large

Directions:

1. Scramble the eggs with some fresh pepper in a large bowl; set aside.
2. Next, over high heat in a small pot, add bone broth a pinch of red pepper flakes. Bring it to a boil, slowly stir in the egg mixture; continue to mix and bring it to a boil again.
3. Remove from the heat and add pepper and salt to taste.
4. Evenly divide the sliced scallions in half, garnish each bowl with. Serve hot enjoy

Nutritional Value: Calories 265; Fat 9g; Carbohydrates 16g; Protein 19.6g

Recipe 17: Fried Egg with Bacon

Serving Size: 1

Cooking Time: 10 minutes

Ingredients:

- 2 eggs
- 30 grams of bacon
- 2 tablespoon olive oil
- Salt
- Pepper

Directions:

1. Heat oil in the pan and fry the bacon.
2. Reduce the heat and beat the eggs in the pan.
3. Cook the eggs and season with salt and pepper.
4. Serve the fried eggs hot with the bacon.

Nutritional Value: Calories 205; Fat 3.8g; Carbohydrates 1g; Protein 8g

Recipe 18: Ground Turkey Stuffed Peppers

Serving Size: 6

Cooking Time: 40 minutes

Ingredients:

- 6 bell peppers
- 1 pound lean ground turkey
- 2 cups mozzarella cheese
- 2 cups brown or basmati rice
- 3 tablespoons taco seasoning

Directions:

1. Prepare the rice per the directions mentioned on the package; set aside let cool.
2. Cut and remove the tops from each bell pepper; get rid of the seeds and membranes.
3. Make few holes towards the bottom of each bell pepper using a toothpick.
4. Stir the cooked rice with ground turkey, 1 ¼ cups of cheese, and taco seasoning in a large-sized mixing bowl.
5. Cook until cooked through or for 10 to 12 minutes, on high pressure.

Nutritional Value: Calories 215; Fat 6.6g; Carbohydrates 14g; Protein 26.6g

Recipe 19: Ham Cheese Omelet

Serving Size: 1

Cooking Time: 5 minutes

Ingredients:

- ⅛ teaspoon pepper
- 4 large egg whites
- 2 teaspoons water
- 2 tablespoons crumbled goat cheese
- 1 slice deli ham, finely chopped
- 2 tablespoons finely chopped green pepper
- 2 tablespoons finely chopped onion
- Minced parsley (optional)

Directions:

1. Whisk the egg whites in a mixing bowl. Add the water and pepper; mix well.
2. Add the green pepper, ham, and onion; combine well.
3. Spray some cooking spray on a medium saucepan or skillet and heat it over medium heat.
4. Add the prepared egg mixture and spread evenly to make a round omelet. Cook until the edges are set.
5. Add the goat cheese over one half and fold over the other half.
6. Transfer to a prepared serving plate, slice, and serve warm with minced parsley on top (optional).

Nutritional Value: Calories 143; Fat 4g; Carbohydrates 5g; Protein 21g

Recipe 20: Hardboiled Egg Prawns

Serving Size: 2

Cooking Time: 15 minutes

Ingredients:

- 4 eggs
- 8 large king prawns, cooked, peeled
- 1 tablespoon mayonnaise, low fat
- 1 teaspoon of paprika
- 1 tablespoon dill or chives, chopped

Directions:

1. Place the king prawns and eggs into a steamer, then boil until eggs are fully hardened, and prawns are ready. Transfer to a container filled with ice water and begin to plunge. Peel each egg when they are cool enough.
2. Slice in half (lengthways), then scoop out the yolks. Mash the yolks, mayonnaise, and paprika together with a fork.
3. Load the paprika mash back into the egg halves, place a king prawn on top of each (use the mash to secure it) and sprinkle with the dill (chopped).
4. Season with a generous amount of salt as well as pepper and serve.

Nutritional Value: Calories 199; Fat 13g; Carbohydrates 5g; Protein 16g

Recipe 21: Lavender Blueberry Chia Seed Pudding

Serving Size: 4

Cooking Time: 0 minutes

Ingredients:

- 100 g blueberries
- 70 g organic quark
- 50 g soy yogurt
- 30 g hazelnuts
- 200 ml almond milk
- 2 tablespoon chia seeds
- 2 teaspoons agave syrup
- 2 teaspoons of lavender

Directions:

1. Bring the almond milk to a boil alongside the lavender.
2. Let the mixture simmer for 10 minutes at a reduced temperature.
3. Allow them to calm down afterward.
4. If the milk is cold, add the blueberries and puree everything.
5. Mix the entire thing with the chia seeds and agave syrup.
6. Let everything soak in the refrigerator for an hour.
7. Mix the yogurt and curd cheese.
8. Add both to the crowd.
9. Divide the pudding into glasses.
10. Finely chop the hazelnuts and sprinkle them on top..

Nutritional Value: Calories 252; Fat 2g; Carbohydrates 11g; Protein 8g

Recipe 22: Pancakes with Berries

Serving Size: 2

Cooking Time: 20 minutes

Ingredients:

- 1 egg
- 50 g spelled flour
- 50 g almond flour
- 15 g coconut flour 150 ml of water salt

Directions:

1. Put the flour, egg, and a few salts in a blender jar.
2. Add 150 ml of water.
3. Mix everything with a whisk.
4. Mix everything into a batter.
5. Heat a coated pan.
6. Put in half the batter.
7. Once the pancake is firm, turn it over.
8. Remove the pancake, add the last half of the batter to the pan, and repeat.
9. Melt chocolate over a water bath.
10. Let the pancakes cool.
11. Brush the pancakes with the yogurt.
12. Wash the berry and let it drain.
13. Put berries on the yogurt.
14. Roll up the pancakes.
15. Sprinkle them with granulated sugar.
16. Decorate the entire thing with the melted chocolate.

Nutritional Value: Calories 298; Fat 9g; Carbohydrates 26g; Protein 21g

Recipe 23: Pecan Oats Pancakes

Serving Size: 6

Cooking Time: 15 minutes

Ingredients:

- ⅓ cup skim milk
- ⅓ cup mashed banana (about ½ medium banana)
- ½ teaspoon vanilla extract
- 2 tablespoons chopped pecans
- 1 tablespoon canola oil
- 1 cup quick-cooking oats
- 1½ teaspoons baking powder
- 2 eggs, beaten

Directions:

1. Add the oats to a prepared blender or food processor and blend to make a flour-like powder.
2. In a bowl, combine the oat powder with the baking powder.
3. In another bowl, combine the beaten eggs, banana, milk and vanilla.
4. Combine the mixtures and mix well. Mix in the pecans.
5. Add the canola oil to a medium saucepan or skillet and heat it over medium heat.
6. Add ¼ of the mixture and spread it into a round shape.
7. Cook on both sides until golden brown. Repeat with the remaining batter.
8. Serve warm.

Nutritional Value: Calories 130; Fat 7g; Carbohydrates 13g; Protein 5g

Recipe 24: Potato Hash

Serving Size: 4

Cooking Time: 15 minutes

Ingredients:

- A drizzle of olive oil
- 2 gold potatoes, cubed
- 2 garlic cloves, minced
- 1 yellow onion, chopped
- 1 cup canned chickpeas, drained
- Salt and black pepper to the taste
- 1 and ½ teaspoon allspice, ground
- 1-pound baby asparagus, trimmed and chopped
- 1 teaspoon sweet paprika
- 1 teaspoon oregano, dried
- 1 teaspoon coriander, ground
- 2 tomatoes, cubed
- 1 cup parsley, chopped
- ½ cup feta cheese, crumbled

Directions:

1. Heat a skillet over medium-high heat with a splash of oil, add the potatoes, onion, garlic, salt, and pepper, and cook for 7 minutes.
2. Toss in the other ingredients, except the tomatoes, parsley, and cheese, and cook for another 7 minutes before transferring to a dish.
3. Add the remaining ingredients, toss and serve for breakfast.

Nutritional Value: Calories 135; Fat 6.6g; Carbohydrates 34g; Protein 26.6g

Recipe 25: Salmon Cakes with Bell Pepper and Lemon Yougurt

Serving Size: 4

Cooking Time: 15 minutes

Ingredients:

- ¼ cup mayonnaise
- 2 tablespoons extra-virgin olive oil
- 1 large egg, beaten
- 1 tablespoon chives, chopped
- 1 tablespoon fresh parsley, chopped
- Zest of 1 lemon
- ¾ teaspoon kosher salt
- 2 (5- to 6-ounce) cans no-salt boneless/skinless salmon
- ¼ teaspoon freshly ground black pepper
- ½ bell pepper, diced small
- 1 cup plain Greek yogurt
- Juice of 1 lemon

Directions:

1. Combine the bread crumbs, mayonnaise, egg, chives, parsley, lemon zest, ½ teaspoon of the salt, plus black pepper in your large bowl, then mix well.
2. Add the salmon and the bell pepper and stir gently until well combined. Shape the mixture into 8 patties.
3. Cook half the cakes until the bottoms are golden brown, 4 to 5 minutes.
4. Combine the yogurt, lemon juice, and the remaining ¼ teaspoon salt in a small bowl, and mix well.
5. Serve with the salmon cakes.

Nutritional Value: Calories 198; Fat 11g; Carbohydrates 16.5g; Protein 20.5g

Recipe 26: Scrambled Eggs

Serving Size: 2

Cooking Time: 25 minutes

Ingredients:

- 2 eggs, scrambled.
- ¼ c. sliced mushrooms.
- ¼ c. chopped onions.
- Olive oil.
- ½ c. young spinach

Directions:

1. Using a pan, add enough olive oil to prevent vegetables from sticking.
2. Add in mushrooms and onions, set heat to low, and fry as you stir until onions become translucent and mushrooms just start to turn green.
3. Add in the spinach, stir before just beginning to wilt. Remove eggs and whisk to mix.
4. Scrape the mixture as they begin to cook. Flip the mixture when the eggs are almost done.
5. Cook to desired moistness/dryness.

Nutritional Value: Calories 199; Fat 13g; Carbohydrates 5g; Protein 16g

Recipe 27: Scrambled Tofu

Serving Size: 4

Cooking Time: 40 minutes

Ingredients:

- ¼ teaspoon onion powder
- 1 c. cherry tomatoes, quartered
- 14 oz. extra-firm tofu
- 1 teaspoon ground turmeric
- 1 teaspoon Olive oil
- ¼ teaspoon garlic powder

Directions:

1. Line a plate with several paper towels. Remove the tofu block from the package and place it on the paper towels.
2. Add additional paper towels to the tofu block and place a cutting board on the paper towels.
3. Weigh the cutting board down with a heavy book, a pot, or several cans.
4. Leave the tofu to drain for at least 30 minutes.
5. In a large sauté pan or skillet, heat the olive oil on medium heat and add the block of tofu.
6. Mash the tofu into small curds with a potato masher.
7. Stir in the turmeric, onion powder, garlic powder, and tomatoes and sauté together for 5 minutes.
8. Serve.

Nutritional Value: Calories 215; Fat 6.6g; Carbohydrates 14g; Protein 26.6g

Recipe 28: Spinach and Egg Bites

Serving Size: 4

Cooking Time: 12 minutes

Ingredients:

- 1 teaspoon turmeric
- ½ teaspoon salt
- 1 c. spinach, roughly chopped
- 2 c. shitake mushrooms, chopped
- 1/3 c. green onions, chopped
- ½ c. nutritional yeast
- 6 eggs
- ½ c. uncooked millet
- 2 c. water
- 1 large clove garlic, peeled and pressed
- 1 c. coconut milk
- ½ teaspoon pepper

Directions:

1. Preheat the oven to 350 degrees F. Oil muffin tins.
2. Using a medium pot, set over medium-high heat, toast in the millet as you stir occasionally.
3. Add salt and water. Increase the heat and allow to boil while covered. Slightly lower the intensity of the heat to continue cooking until the water is completely absorbed.
4. In a bowl, whisk pepper, eggs, salt, turmeric, coconut milk, and garlic. Toss in mushrooms, green onions, spinach, and millet.
5. Spoon the mixture into muffin cups; bake for 12 minutes.
6. Once the egg bites are removed from the oven, sprinkle with nutritional yeast. Let cool slightly before you serve.

Nutritional Value: Calories 199; Fat 13g; Carbohydrates 5g; Protein 16g

Recipe 29: Tofu Tomato Breakfast

Serving Size: 2

Cooking Time: 10 minutes

Ingredients:

- 1 medium green bell pepper, chopped
- ½ medium red onion, chopped
- 1 pound firm tofu, drained and crumbled
- 1 tomato, seeded and chopped
- ½ teaspoon turmeric (optional)
- ½ teaspoon salt
- 1 teaspoon cumin powder
- ¼ teaspoon chili powder
- 1 teaspoon garlic powder
- 1 tablespoon water
- Chopped coriander and lemon juice to garnish

Directions:

1. Grease a medium prepared saucepan or skillet with some actual cooking spray and heat it over medium heat.
2. Add the prepared onion, tomato, and bell pepper and stir cook for 2–3 minutes until softened.
3. Stir in the crumbled tofu and spices; add some water if needed and stir-cook for 2–3 minutes until the mixture becomes fragrant. Season to taste and cook until the tofu is scrambled.
4. Serve with fresh lemon juice on top.

Nutritional Value: Calories 238; Fat 11g; Carbohydrates 16.5g; Protein 20.5g

Recipe 30: Veggie and Bacon Hash with Egg Nests

Serving Size: 2

Cooking Time: 25 minutes

Ingredients:

- 1 avocado, sliced
- 2 bacon slices, chopped
- ½ teaspoon smoked paprika
- ½ head cauliflower, cut into ¼-inch dice
- ½ teaspoon freshly ground black pepper
- ½ zucchini, cut into ½-inch cubes
- ½ white onion, chopped
- ½ red bell pepper, cut into ½-inch squares
- ⅓ cup sweet potato, cut into ¼-inch dice
- ½ teaspoon sea salt
- 4 large eggs

Directions:

1. In a medium skillet, cook the bacon until slightly crispy. Remove from the pan and place on a plate lined with paper towels.
2. Add the cauliflower, zucchini, onion, bell pepper, sweet potato, smoked paprika, salt, and black pepper. Cook for 8 to 10 minutes, occasionally stirring until the vegetables become tender and golden. Return the bacon to the pan.
3. Make 4 holes in the hash and crack an egg into each hole. Cover and cook for 5 minutes, or until your desired doneness of the egg is reached.
4. Divide evenly between two plates and garnish with avocado slices.

Nutritional Value: Calories 135; Fat 6.6g; Carbohydrates 34g; Protein 26.6g

Chapter 3: Lunch Recipes

Recipe 31: Black Bean Patties with Cilantro

Serving Size: 4

Cooking Time: 10 minutes

Ingredients:

- 2 whole wheat bread slices, torn
- 3 tablespoons of cilantro, chopped
- 2 garlic cloves, minced
- 15 ounces of canned black beans, no-salt-added, drained and rinsed
- 6 ounces of canned chipotle peppers, chopped
- 1 teaspoon of cumin, ground
- 1 egg
- Cooking spray
- ½ avocado, peeled, pitted, and mashed
- 1 tablespoon of lime juice
- 1 cherry tomato, chopped

Directions:

1. Pulse the bread until it is finely crushed in a food processor. Transfer the bread crumbs to a large mixing basin.
2. Stir thoroughly and form 4 patties out of the mixture once combined with the cilantro, garlic, black beans, chipotle peppers, cumin, and egg.
3. Heat a skillet over medium-high heat and oil with cooking spray before adding the bean patties and frying them for 5 minutes on each side before transferring them to plates. 4.
4. In a large mixing bowl, combine the avocado, tomato, and lime juice, stirring well to incorporate. Spread the mixture over the patties and serve for lunch.
5. Enjoy!

Nutritional Value: Calories 200; Fat 4g; Carbohydrates 12g; Protein 8g

Recipe 32: Braised Chicken Wings

Serving Size: 8

Cooking Time: 40 minutes

Ingredients:

- 24 pcs chicken wings, split
- ½ cup dark soy sauce, divided
- 3 tablespoon ginger, thinly sliced and divided
- 3 pcs scallions, trimmed and halved crosswise
- 1 pc shallot, thinly sliced
- 5 cloves garlic, smashed
- 1 pc Fresno chili, halved lengthwise
- 2 teaspoon five spice powder, divided
- ¼ cup unseasoned rice wine
- 3 pcs whole star anise
- 1 pc cinnamon stick
- ½ cup low-sodium soy sauce
- ¼ teaspoon Sichuan peppercorns
- 3 tablespoon vegetable oil
- 1 cup water
- ¼ cup sugar
- ¼ teaspoon freshly ground white pepper

Directions:

1. Toss chicken together with dark soy sauce, plus half of ginger and five spice powder. Set aside to marinade in the fridge for about an hour.
2. Heat oil in a wok on medium high when the chicken wings are ready and stir fry scallions, shallots, garlic, and remaining ginger. Stir for about 2 minutes, then, sprinkle sugar, star anise, cinnamon stick, peppercorns, and white pepper.
3. Pour in the remaining dark soy sauce, plus low-sodium soy sauce, plus water, and let it boil on high.
4. Add chicken wings, discarding marinade, and pour vinegar. Turn heat to low and simmer for about 30 minutes, covered, stirring occasionally.
5. Remove wings to a plate with a slotted spoon and pour the liquid through a fine sieve, discarding solids.
6. Return the liquid to a saucepan and simmer on high until thickened and reduced.
7. Put back the chicken wings into the sauce, toss gently, and transfer to a serving platter.
8. Serve and enjoy.

Nutritional Value: Calories 264; Fat 9.3g; Carbohydrates 2.3g; Protein 1.2g

Recipe 33: Cajun Garlic Shrimp Noodle Bowl

Serving Size: 2

Cooking Time: 15 minutes

Ingredients:

- ½ teaspoon salt
- 1 onion, sliced
- 1 red pepper, sliced
- 1 tablespoon butter
- 1 teaspoon garlic granules
- 1 teaspoon onion powder
- 1 teaspoon paprika
- 2 large zucchinis, cut into noodle strips
- 20 jumbo shrimps, shells removed and deveined
- 3 cloves garlic, minced
- 3 tablespoon ghee
- A dash of cayenne pepper
- A dash of red pepper flake

Directions:

1. Preparation are the Cajun seasoning by mixing the onion powder, garlic granules, pepper flakes, cayenne pepper, paprika and salt. Toss in the shrimp to coat in the seasoning.
2. In a skillet, heat the ghee and sauté the garlic. Add in the red pepper and onions and continue sautéing for 4 minutes.
3. Add the Cajun shrimp and cook until opaque. Set aside.
4. In another pan, heat the butter and sauté the zucchini noodles for three minutes.
5. Assemble by the placing the Cajun shrimps on top of the zucchini noodles.

Nutritional Value: Calories 512; Fat 30g; Carbohydrates 20.2g; Protein 9.7g

Recipe 34: Cheesy Lamb Burgers

Serving Size: 4

Preparation Time: 15 minutes

Cooking Time: 20 minutes

Ingredients:

- 2 pounds of ground lamb
- 1 cup of Parmigiano-Reggiano cheese, grated
- Salt and ground black pepper, to taste

Directions:

1. Set the temperature of the Grill to 425 degrees F and preheat with a closed lid for 15 minutes.
2. Combine all ingredients in a bowl.
3. Make 4 (¾-inch thick) patties from the mixture.
4. Make a small but broad indentation in each patty with your thumbs.
5. Place the patties, depression-side down, on the grill and cook for approximately 8 minutes.
6. Flip and cook for about 8-10 minutes.
7. Serve immediately.

Nutritional Value: Calories 206; Fat 9g; Carbohydrates 26.3g; Protein 10.2g

Recipe 35: Chicken Garlic Roast

Serving Size: 4

Cooking Time: 25 minutes

Ingredients:

- 4 pieces grass-fed chicken thighs
- 4 cloves garlic
- 4 stems rosemary
- 3 tablespoon extra-virgin olive oil
- 1 lemon
- ¼ teaspoon ground black pepper
- ½ cup organic chicken stock

Directions:

1. Preheat oven to 450 degrees.
2. Strip the leaves from the rosemary and crush the garlic. Grate the lemon into zest and juice and separate the two.
3. Place chicken on a baking dish. Add garlic, rosemary, lemon zest, olive oil, and ground black pepper. Toss chicken to coat thoroughly and roast (uncovered) for 20 minutes.
4. After 20 minutes of roasting, add chicken broth and lemon juice. Turn over chicken.
5. Return to oven, turn the oven off, and let sit 5 minutes longer.
6. Remove from oven and place on a serving dish, pouring pan juices over the chicken. Serve immediately or chill for 20 minutes and serve.

Nutritional Value: Calories 379; Fat 19.9g; Carbohydrates 23.9g; Protein 7.6g

Recipe 36: Chicken Kebabs

Serving Size: 4

Cooking Time: 20 minutes

Ingredients:

- 2 chicken breasts, skinless, boneless, and cubed
- 1 red bell pepper, cut into squares
- 1 red onion, roughly cut into squares
- 2 teaspoons sweet paprika
- 1 teaspoon nutmeg, ground
- 1 teaspoon Italian seasoning
- ¼ teaspoon smoked paprika
- A pinch of salt and black pepper
- ¼ teaspoon cardamom, ground
- Juice of 1 lemon
- 3 garlic cloves, minced
- ½ cup olive oil

Directions:

1. Combine the chicken with the onion, the bell pepper, and the other ingredients, toss well, cover the bowl and keep in the fridge for 30 minutes.
2. Assemble skewers with chicken, peppers, and onions, place them on your preheated grill and cook over medium heat for 8 minutes on each side.
3. Divide the kebabs between plates and serve with a side salad.

Nutritional Value: Calories 262; Fat 14g; Carbohydrates 14g; Protein 20g

Recipe 37: Chipotle Adobo Chicken

Serving Size: 6

Cooking Time: 20 minutes

Ingredients:

- 2 lbs chicken thighs or breasts

For the marinade:

- ¼ cup olive oil
- 2 chipotle peppers, in adobo sauce
- 1 tablespoon garlic, minced
- 1 shallot, finely chopped
- 1 ½ tablespoons cumin
- 1 tablespoon cilantro, super-finely chopped or dried
- 2 teaspoons chili powder
- 1 teaspoon dried oregano
- 1/2 teaspoon salt
- Fresh limes, garnish
- Cilantro, garnish

Directions:

1. Preheat griddle to medium-high.
2. Add the prepared marinade ingredients to a food processor or blender and pulse into a paste.
3. Add the chicken and marinade to a sealable plastic bag and massage to coat well.
4. Place in the refrigerator for approximately about 1 hour to 24 hours before cooking.
5. Sear chicken for 7 minutes, turn and cook and additional 7 minutes.
6. Turn heat to low and continue to cook until chicken has reached an internal temperature of 165°F.
7. Remove chicken from griddle and allow to rest 5 to 10 minutes before serving.
8. Garnish with a prepared squeeze of fresh lime and a sprinkle of cilantro to serve.

Nutritional Value: Calories 200; Fat 4g; Carbohydrates 12g; Protein 8g

Recipe 38: Chutney Curry Chicken Wings

Serving Size: 5

Cooking Time: 35 minutes

Ingredients:

- 2 & 1/2 lbs. of chicken wings
- 4 tablespoon of curry powder, organic
- 2 teaspoon of salt, pink Himalayan
- 2/3 cup of chutney, mango
- 2 tablespoon of Worcestershire sauce, reduced sodium
- 2 tablespoon of oyster sauce, bottled

Directions:

1. Place wings in zipper top bag. Season with Himalayan salt & organic curry powder. Shake well. Be sure all wings are coated well with the seasonings.
2. In medium bowl, combine mango chutney, oyster sauce and Worcestershire sauce. Pour over the wings, coating each one. Then, place bag in refrigerator and allow to chill for 1/2 hour to three hours. You can also let them marinate overnight, if you like.
3. Remove bag from refrigerator. Place wings on cookie sheet lined with parchment paper. Leave some space between them. Spoon marinade over wings.
4. Bake in 400F oven for 20-25 minutes, till cooked fully through. Serve.

Nutritional Value: Calories 200; Fat 4g; Carbohydrates 12g; Protein 8g

Recipe 39: Crispy Onion Wings

Serving Size: 12

Cooking Time: 45 minutes

Ingredients:

- 12 whole chicken wings (about 2-1/2 lbs.)
- 2-1/2 cups crushed potato chips
- 1 can (2.8 oz.) french-fried onions, crushed
- 1/2 cup cornmeal
- 2 teaspoons dried oregano
- 1 teaspoon onion salt
- 1 teaspoon garlic powder
- 1 teaspoon paprika
- 2 large eggs
- 1/4 cup butter, melted

Directions:

1. Line a foil into a 15x10x1-inch baking pan and coat the foil with oil; put aside. Slice chicken wings into 3 portions; dispose of the wing tip portions.
2. Mix seasonings, cornmeal, onions, and potato chips together in a big resealable plastic bag. Whisk eggs in a shallow bowl. In the eggs, dip the chicken wings. In the bag, put the shrimp, several each time. Close the bag and shake to coat; press into the chicken with the crumb mixture.
3. In the prepared pan, put the wings; drizzle butter over. Bake without a cover at 375° until the coating is crunchy and the chicken juices run clear, about 30-35 minutes.

Nutritional Value: Calories 206; Fat 8g; Carbohydrates 26.3g; Protein 10.2g

Recipe 40: Crispy Pollock and Gazpacho

Serving Size: 3

Cooking Time: 15 minutes

Ingredients:

- 85 g whole-wheat bread, torn into chunks
- 4 tablespoons olive oil
- 4 pieces Pollock fillets, skinless
- 4 large tomatoes, cut into chunks
- 3/4 cucumber, cut into chunks
- 2 tablespoons sherry vinegar
- 2 garlic cloves, crushed
- 1/2 red onion, thinly sliced
- 1 yellow pepper, deseeded, cut into chunks

Directions:

1. Preheat the oven to 200C, gas to 6, or fan to 180C.
2. Over a baking tray, scatter the chunks of bread. Toss with 1 tablespoon of the prepared olive oil and bake for about 10 minutes, or until golden and crispy.
3. Meanwhile, mix the cucumber, tomatoes, onion, pepper, crushed garlic, sherry vinegar, and 2 tablespoons of the olive oil; season well.
4. Heat a non-stick large frying pan. Add the remaining prepared 1 tablespoon of the olive oil and heat. When the prepared oil is already hot, add the fish; cook for about 4 minutes or until golden. Flip the fillet; cook for additional 1 to 2 minutes or until the fish cooked through.
5. In a mixing bowl, quickly toss the salad and the croutons; divide among 4 plates and then serve with the fish.

Nutritional Value: Calories 296; Fat 13g; Carbohydrates 19g; Protein 27g

Recipe 41: Cuban Pork Chops

Serving Size: 4

Cooking Time: 1 hour 30 minutes

Ingredients:

- 4 pork chops
- 4 cloves garlic, smashed
- 2 tablespoons olive oil
- 1/3 cup lime juice
- 1/4 cup water
- 1 teaspoon ground cumin
- Salt and black pepper

Directions:

1. Set your griddle to medium. Salt the pork chops on both side and cook the chops until lightly browned.
2. Combine the water, garlic, and lime juice in a bowl and whisk until even.
3. Continue cooking the pork chops while basting them with the lime juice mixture.
4. When the prepared pork chops have finished cooking, remove from the griddle and top with additional sauce and black pepper before serving.

Nutritional Value: Calories 264; Fat 9.3g; Carbohydrates 2.3g; Protein 1.2g

Recipe 42: Garbanzo Bean Burger

Serving Size: 4

Cooking Time: 40 minutes

Ingredients:

Cutlet:

- 1/2 cup of diced Kale
- 1 cup of Garbanzo Bean Flour
- 1/2 cup of minced Onions
- 2 teaspoons of Onion Powder
- 2 teaspoons of Oregano
- 1 diced Plum Tomato
- 2 teaspoons of Basil
- 1 teaspoon of Dill
- 1/2 cup of diced Green Peppers
- 1/2 teaspoon of Cayenne
- 2 teaspoons of Pure Sea Salt
- 1/2 teaspoon of Cayenne Powder
- 2 tablespoons of Grape Seed Oil
- 1/2 cup of Spring Water

Burger:

- 8 Flatbreads
- 2 sliced Plum Tomatoes
- 1 sliced Red Onion
- 1 cup of sauce

Directions:

1. Mix all vegetables and seasonings in a large bowl.
2. Add the Garbanzo Bean Flour to it and mix well.
3. Slowly pour Spring Water and mix thoroughly until it can be easily shaped into cutlets. If it's too loose, add more flour.
4. Add Grape Seed Oil to a skillet and warm it on high heat.
5. Reduce to medium heat. Place the formed cutlets in the pan and cook for about 2 to 3 minutes on all sides until golden brown.
6. Take one Flatbread and put the cooked burger cutlet on it. Add greens, sliced Tomatoes, Onions, and any sauce from our recipes.
7. Serve and enjoy your Garbanzo Bean Burger!

Nutritional Value: Calories 379; Fat 19.9g; Carbohydrates 23.9g; Protein 7.6g

Recipe 43: Garlic Parsley Prawn Skewers

Serving Size: 5

Cooking Time: 8 minutes

Ingredients:

- ¼ cup fresh parsley leaves, minced
- 1 tablespoon garlic, crushed
- 2½ tablespoons olive oil
- 2 tablespoons Thai chili sauce
- 1 tablespoon fresh lime juice
- 1½ pounds prawns, peeled and deveined

Directions:

1. In a large-sized bowl, add all ingredients except for prawns and mix well.
2. In a resealable plastic bag, add marinade and prawns.
3. Seal the prepared bag and shake to coat well
4. Refrigerate for approximately about 20-30 minutes.
5. Preheat the griddle to 450 degrees F.
6. Remove the prawns from marinade and thread onto metal skewers.
7. Arrange the skewers onto the griddle and cook for about 4 minutes per side.
8. Remove the skewers from griddle and serve hot.

Nutritional Value: Calories 234; Fat 9.3g; Carbohydrates 4.9g; Protein 31.2g

Recipe 44: Hasselback Stuffed Chicken

Serving Size: 4

Cooking Time: 30 minutes

Ingredients:

- 4 boneless, skinless chicken breasts
- 2 tablespoons olive oil
- 2 tablespoons taco seasoning
- 1/2 red, yellow and green pepper, very thinly sliced
- 1 small red onion, very thinly sliced
- 1/2 cup Mexican shredded cheese
- Guacamole, for serving
- Sour cream, for serving
- Salsa, for serving

Directions:

1. Preheat griddle to med-high.
2. Cut thin horizontal cuts across each chicken breast; like you would hasselback potatoes.
3. Rub chicken evenly with olive oil and taco seasoning.
4. Add a mixture of bell peppers and red onions to each cut, and place the breasts on the griddle.
5. Cook chicken for 15 minutes.
6. Remove and top with cheese.
7. Tent loosely with foil and cook another 5 minutes, until cheese is melted.
8. Remove from griddle and top with guacamole, sour cream and salsa. Serve alongside your favorite side dishes!

Nutritional Value: Calories 643; Fat 18.6g; Carbohydrates 26.3g; Protein 9.3g

Recipe 45: Juicy Steamed Garlic Halibut

Serving Size: 4

Cooking Time: 25 minutes

Ingredients:

- 1 pound halibut fillet
- 1 lemon, freshly squeezed
- 1 tablespoon dill weed, chopped
- 1 teaspoon garlic powder
- Salt and pepper to taste

Directions:

1. Take a large pot and fill it up with 1.5 inches of water.
2. Place it over medium heat.
3. Place a trivet inside the pot.
4. Take a baking dish small enough to fit inside the pot.
5. Add listed ingredients and gently stir.
6. Cover the baking dish with foil.
7. Place it over the top of the trivet inside the pot.
8. Cover the pot and steam fish for 15 minutes.
9. Keep the fish for 10 minutes before removing it from the pot.
10. Serve and enjoy!

Nutritional Value: Calories 200; Fat 4g; Carbohydrates 12g; Protein 8g

Recipe 46: Lemon and Butter Cod

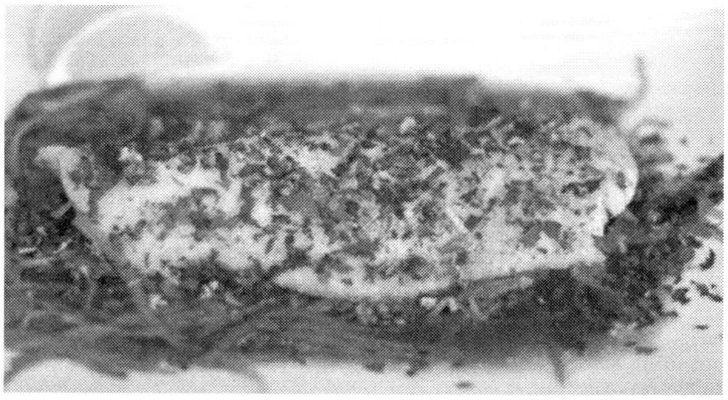

Serving Size: 3

Cooking Time: 20 minutes

Ingredients:

- 4 tablespoons salted almond butter, divided
- 4 thyme sprigs, fresh and divided
- 4 teaspoons lemon juice, fresh and divided
- 4 cod fillets, 6 ounces each
- Salt to taste

Directions:

1. Preheat your oven to 400 degrees F.
2. Season cod fillets with salt on both sides.
3. Cut four pieces of foil, each one three times the size of the fillets.
4. Place the fillets on foil and cover with butter, lemon juice, and thyme.
5. Fold the pouches in half and place them on a baking pan.
6. Bake for 20 minutes.
7. Open and let the steam out.
8. Serve and enjoy!

Nutritional Value: Calories 200; Fat 4g; Carbohydrates 12g; Protein 8g

Recipe 47: Marinated Mushroom Kabobs

Serving Size: 4

Cooking Time: 10 minutes

Ingredients:

- 1 onion, cut into 2-inch pieces
- 1 green pepper, 2-inch pieces
- 1-pint of cherry tomatoes
- 1 punnet white button mushrooms, whole
- 1 yellow pepper, 2-inch pieces

For the marinade:

- 2 cloves of garlic, minced
- 1/2 teaspoon of dried oregano
- 1/4 cup of olive oil
- 1 lemon, juiced
- 1/2 teaspoon of sea salt

Directions:

1. Arrange vegetables in an alternating pattern on metal skewers.
2. Place onto a baking sheet or a piece of aluminum foil to catch the drips.
3. In a prepared small-sized mixing bowl, whisk together the marinade ingredients & pour on skewers; turn skewers to coat well.
4. Preheat your Blackstone griddle at medium and apply the thin layer of olive oil on the griddle. Cook the steaks for around 4 to 5 minutes on each side till browned.
5. Place the kabobs on a serving platter and serve!

Nutritional Value: Calories 173; Fat 13g; Carbohydrates 16g; Protein 3g

Recipe 48: Marinated Pork Shoulder

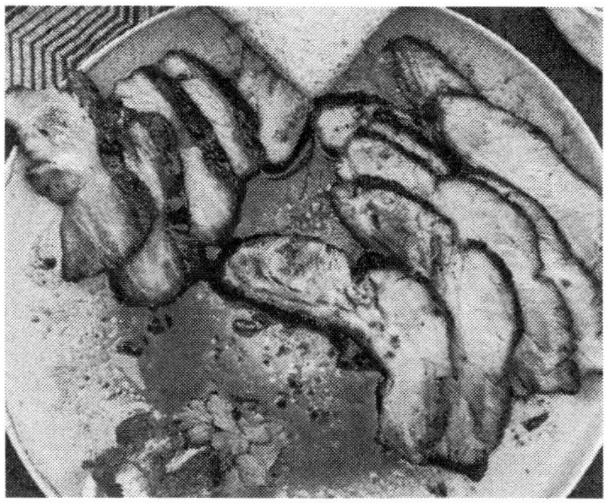

Serving Size: 8

Cooking Time: 8 minutes

Ingredients:

- 1 (5 lbs.) Boston Butt pork shoulder

For the marinade:

- 2 tablespoons garlic, minced
- 1 large piece ginger, peeled and chopped
- 1 cup hoisin sauce
- ¾ cup fish sauce
- ⅔ cup honey
- ⅔ cup Shaoxing
- ½ cup chili oil
- ⅓ cup oyster sauce
- ⅓ cup sesame oil

For the glaze:

- ¾ cup dark brown sugar
- 1 tablespoon light molasses

Directions:

1. A cutting board with the actual short end facing you is ideal for pork shoulder. Make a shallow incision along the length of a long side of shoulder with a long sharp knife approximately 1"–112" above the cutting board. Cut further into the meat, raising and unfurling it with your free hand. Purée marinade in a blender and reserve 1 ½ cups for glaze, cover and refrigerate. Pour remaining marinade in a large sealable plastic bag. Add pork shoulder to bag and marinate in the refrigerator for 8 hours.
2. Preheat griddle to medium heat (with cover closed, thermometer should register 350°). Remove the pork from the marinade, allowing any extra liquid to drop out. Add glaze ingredients to reserved marinade until sugar is dissolved. Griddle pork for 8 minutes, basting and flipping with tongs every minute or two, until thickly covered with glaze, lightly seared in areas, and warmed through. Transfer to an actual cutting board and slice against the grain, ¼" thick, to serve.

Nutritional Value: Calories 486; Fat 8.4g; Carbohydrates 53g; Protein 8.7g

Recipe 49: Oyster Stew

Serving Size: 6

Cooking Time: 1 hour and 10 minutes

Ingredients:

- 2 garlic cloves, minced
- ¼ cup jarred roasted red peppers
- 2 teaspoons oregano, chopped
- 1-pound lamb meat, ground
- 1 tablespoon red wine vinegar
- Salt and black pepper to the taste
- 1 teaspoon red pepper flakes
- 2 tablespoons olive oil
- 1 and ½ cups chicken stock
- 36 oysters, shucked
- 1 and ½ cups canned black-eyed peas, drained

Directions:

1. Heat the oil in a saucepan over medium heat, add the meat and garlic and cook for 5 minutes.
2. Add the peppers and the rest of the ingredients, bring to a simmer and cook for 15 minutes.
3. Divide the stew into bowls and serve.

Nutritional Value: Calories 264; Fat 9.3g; Carbohydrates 2.3g; Protein 1.2g

Recipe 50: Salmon Panatela

Serving Size: 4

Cooking Time: 22 minutes

Ingredients:

- 1 lb skinned salmon, cut into 4 steaks each
- 1 cucumber, peeled, seeded, cubed
- Salt and black pepper to taste
- 8 black olives, pitted and chopped
- 1 tablespoon capers, rinsed
- 2 large tomatoes, diced
- 3 tablespoon red wine vinegar
- ¼ cup thinly sliced red onion
- 3 tablespoon olive oil
- 2 slices zero carb bread, cubed
- ¼ cup thinly sliced basil leaves

Directions:

1. Preheat a grill to 350°F and preparation are the salad. In a bowl, mix the cucumbers, olives, pepper, capers, tomatoes, wine vinegar, onion, olive oil, bread, and basil leaves. Let sit for the flavors to incorporate.
2. Season the prepared salmon steaks with salt and pepper; grill them on both sides for 8 minutes in total. Serve the salmon steaks warm on a bed of the veggies' salad.

Nutritional Value: Calories 338; Fat 27g; Carbohydrates 10g; Protein 25g

Recipe 51: Sauteed Chorizo

Serving Size: 4

Cooking Time: 13 minutes

Ingredients:

- 1 and 1.2 cups soft chorizo, sliced
- 3 tablespoons olive oil
- 1/3 cup dry red wine
- White bread, cubed

Directions:

1. In a hot skillet, sauté the chorizo for 4 minutes, turning periodically.
2. Stir and cook for 5 minutes. Add wine, stir, and simmer for 3 minutes.
3. Pour this into bowls and serve with cubed bread on top.

Nutritional Value: Calories 340; Fat 23g; Carbohydrates 2g; Protein 21g

Recipe 52: Savory Bacon Pork Chops with Pineapple

Serving Size: 6

Cooking Time: 1 hour

Ingredients:

- 1 large whole pineapple
- 6 pork chops
- 12 slices thick-cut bacon
- Toothpicks, soaked in water

For the glaze:

- ¼ cup honey
- ⅛ teaspoon cayenne pepper

Directions:

1. Turn both burners to medium-high heat; after approximately about 15 minutes, turn off one of the middle burners and then, turn the remaining burners down to medium.
2. Slice off the top and bottom of the pineapple, and peel the pineapple, cutting the skin off in strips. Cut pineapple flesh into six quarters.
3. Wrap each pineapple section with a bacon slice; secure each end with a toothpick.
4. Brush quarters with honey and sprinkle with cayenne pepper. Put the quarters on the griddle, flipping when bacon is cooked so that both sides are evenly Griddle.
5. While pineapple quarters are cooking, coat pork chops with honey and cayenne pepper. Set on griddle.
6. Tent with foil and cook for 20 minutes. Flip, and continue cooking an additional 10 to 20 minutes or until chops are fully cooked. Serve each chop with a pineapple quarter on the side.

Nutritional Value: Calories 380; Fat 23.5g; Carbohydrates 18.2g; Protein 25.8g

Recipe 53: Scallops with Broccoli

Serving Size: 2

Cooking Time: 10 minutes

Ingredients:

- 1 tablespoon olive oil
- 1 cup broccoli, cut into small pieces
- 1 garlic clove, crushed
- ½ pound scallops
- 1 teaspoon fresh lemon juice
- Salt, as required

Directions:

1. Heat oil over medium heat in a large nonstick pan and cook the broccoli and garlic for about 3-4 minutes, stirring occasionally.
2. Put in the scallops and cook within 3-4 minutes, flipping occasionally. Stir in the lemon juice and salt and remove from the heat. Serve hot.

Nutritional Value: Calories 178; Fat 8g; Carbohydrates 6.3g; Protein 20.4g

Recipe 54: Shrimp and Halibut Stew

Serving Size: 6

Cooking Time: 30 minutes

Ingredients:

- 2 garlic cloves, minced
- 2 tablespoons olive oil
- 1 yellow onion, chopped
- 14 ounces canned tomatoes, chopped
- 1 tablespoon orange zest, grated
- 4 and ½ cups seafood stock
- 1-pound halibut fillets, boneless, skinless, and cubed
- 20 shrimp, peeled and deveined
- 1 bunch parsley, chopped
- Salt and white pepper to the taste

Directions:

1. Heat a pot with the oil over medium-high heat, add the onion and the garlic and sauté for 5 minutes.
2. Add the tomatoes, orange zest, and the stock, stir, bring to a boil and simmer for 20 minutes over medium heat.
3. Add the fish and the shrimp, cook for 5 minutes more, divide into bowls, sprinkle the parsley on top, and serve.

Nutritional Value: Calories 300; Fat 14.3g; Carbohydrates 16.1g; Protein 11g

Recipe 55: Shrimp Lunch Rolls

Serving Size: 4

Cooking Time: 0 minutes

Ingredients:

- 12 rice paper sheets, soaked in warm water and drained
- 1 cup of cilantro, chopped
- 12 basil leaves
- 12 baby lettuce leaves
- 1 small cucumber, sliced
- 1 cup of carrots, shredded
- 20 ounces of shrimp, cooked, peeled, and deveined

Directions:

1. Arrange all rice papers on a working surface, divide cilantro, bay leaves, baby lettuce leaves, cucumber, carrots, and shrimp, wrap, seal edges, and serve lunch.
2. Enjoy!

Nutritional Value: Calories 200; Fat 4g; Carbohydrates 14g; Protein 8g

Recipe 56: Spaghetti in Lemon Avocado White Sauce

Serving Size: 3

Cooking Time: 30 minutes

Ingredients:

- Freshly ground black pepper
- Zest and juice of 1 lemon
- 1 avocado, pitted and peeled
- 1-pound spaghetti
- Salt
- 1 tablespoon Olive oil
- 8 oz small shrimp, shelled and deveined
- ¼ cup dry white wine
- 1 large onion, finely sliced

Directions:

1. Let a big pot of water boil. Once boiling add the spaghetti or pasta and cook following manufacturer's instructions until al dente. Drain and set aside.
2. In a large fry pan, over medium fire sauté wine and onions for ten minutes or until onions are translucent and soft.
3. Add the shrimps into the fry pan and increase fire to high while constantly sautéing until shrimps are cooked around five minutes. Turn the fire off. Season with salt and add the oil right away. Then quickly toss in the cooked pasta, mix well.
4. In a blender, until smooth, puree the lemon juice and avocado. Pour into the fry pan of pasta, combine well. Garnish with pepper and lemon zest then serve.

Nutritional Value: Calories 206; Fat 8g; Carbohydrates 26.3g; Protein 10.2g

Recipe 57: Turkey and Asparagus Rolls

Serving Size: 4

Cooking Time: 10 minutes

Ingredients:

- 10 ounces of frozen asparagus spears
- 8 ounces of turkey breast slices
- Black pepper
- Salt

Directions:

1. Place the asparagus in a large bowl and cover them with water, then let it sit for 3 to 5 min then drain it.
2. Wrap each turkey slice on several asparagus spears.
3. Fill 2 inches of a steamer pot with water, then bring it to a boil.
4. Arrange the turkey and asparagus rolls in the steamer basket, place them on the pot, then cover them and steam them for 10 min.
5. Serve your rolls with your favorite dipping sauce and enjoy.

Nutritional Value: Calories 200; Fat 4g; Carbohydrates 12g; Protein 8g

Recipe 58: Turkey Veggie Zoodles

Serving Size: 8

Cooking Time: 40 minutes

Ingredients:

- 1 jalapeno pepper, seeded and chopped
- 1 small onion, finely chopped
- 3 medium zucchini, spiralized
- 1 cup black beans, rinsed and drained
- 2 cloves garlic, minced
- 4 teaspoons olive oil (divided)
- 1 pound ground turkey
- ¼ teaspoon chili powder
- ¼ teaspoon crushed red pepper flakes
- ¾ teaspoon ground cumin
- ¼ teaspoon pepper
- ½ teaspoon salt
- 1 cup corn kernels
- 4 plum tomatoes, chopped
- Chopped cilantro and shredded cheddar cheese (optional)

Directions:

1. Heat 2 teaspoons of the prepared olive oil over medium heat in a medium saucepan or skillet. Add the onion, jalapeno and garlic, and stir-cook until softened and translucent.
2. Add the turkey and cook for 8–10 minutes until no longer pinkish. Break the turkey into small pieces. Drain the excess fat.
3. Add the seasoning and combine; set the mixture aside and clean the pan.
4. Heat the remaining oil in the pan. Add the zucchini and stir-cook for 4–5 minutes until softened. Add the beans, tomatoes, corn, and cooked turkey mixture; stir-cook until the beans are cooked to your satisfaction.
5. Serve warm with cheese and cilantro on top.

Nutritional Value: Calories 332; Fat 14g; Carbohydrates 26g; Protein 29g

Recipe 59: White Pizza with Broccoli Crust

Serving Size: 2

Cooking Time: 35 minutes

Ingredients:

- 2 1/2 cups broccoli (riced)
- 1 egg
- 1/3 cup + ¾ cup shredded mozzarella cheese (low-fat)
- 1/4 cup grated Parmesan cheese
- 1/2 teaspoon Italian seasoning
- 1/2 cup ricotta cheese (part-skim)
- 1/4 teaspoon red pepper flakes
- 1 garlic clove (minced)
- 1/2 cup broccoli florets (chopped)

Directions:

1. Preheat oven to 400°F.
2. Cook broccoli in a microwave-safe tray and then cover it (about 3 minutes).
3. Once cooled, transfer "rice" to a cheesecloth or clean, thin dishtowel and squeezed out as much liquid as possible.
4. Take a bowl, mix in broccoli, egg, one-third cup Mozzarella cheese, Parmesan cheese, and Italian seasoning, and combine well.
5. Form mixture into a square pizza (1/3 inch thick) onto a baking sheet. Bake until edges are brown (15-20 minutes).
6. Meanwhile, take a bowl, combine ricotta, red pepper flakes, and garlic, and then spread this ricotta mixture onto broccoli crust, sprinkle with the remaining mozzarella, and top with broccoli. Bake for an additional until cheese is melted (about 5-10 minutes).

Nutritional Value: Calories 279; Fat 16.7g; Carbohydrates 9.5g; Protein 23.8g

Recipe 60: Yellow Curry Chicken Wings

Serving Size: 6

Cooking Time: 45 minutes

Ingredients:

- 2 lbs. chicken wings

For the marinade:

- 1/2 cup Greek yogurt, plain
- 1 tablespoon mild yellow curry powder
- 1 tablespoon olive oil
- ½ teaspoon sea salt
- ½ teaspoon black pepper
- 1 teaspoon red chili flakes

Directions:

1. Rinse and then pat wings dry with paper towels.
2. Whisk all of the prepared marinade ingredients together in a large mixing bowl until well-combined.
3. Add wings to medium-sized bowl and toss to coat.
4. Cover the medium-sized bowl with plastic wrap and chill in the refrigerator for 30 minutes.
5. Prepare one side of the griddle for medium heat and the other side on medium-high.
6. Working in batches, grill wings over medium heat, turning occasionally, until skin starts to brown; about 12 minutes.
7. Move wings to medium-high area of griddle for 5 minutes on each side to char until cooked through; meat thermometer should register 165°F when touching the bone.
8. Transfer wings to a platter and serve warm.

Nutritional Value: Calories 371; Fat 21g; Carbohydrates 15g; Protein 7.8g

Chapter 4: Dinner Recipes

Recipe 61: Barbecue Ribs

Serving Size: 4

Cooking Time: 12 hours

Ingredients:

- 1 rack pork ribs
- 1 tablespoon salt
- 1 teaspoon pepper
- 2 tablespoons natural stevia
- 1 tablespoon garlic powder
- 1 tablespoon onion powder
- 2 tablespoons paprika
- ½ cup barbecue sauce, plus extra for serving

Directions:

1. Preheat the water bath to 165 degrees F.
2. Combine salt, pepper, stevia, garlic powder, onion powder, and paprika.
3. Rub all over ribs. Seal ribs into bag and place in water bath. Cook 12 hours.
4. When ribs are cooked, place on a baking sheet lined with aluminum foil.
5. Spread barbecue sauce over ribs. Place under broiler until sauce bubbles.
6. Serve with additional sauce.

Nutritional Value: Calories 379; Fat 19.9g; Carbohydrates 23.9g; Protein 7.6g

Recipe 62: Brandy Roast Beef

Serving Size: 4

Preparation Time: 20 minutes

Cooking Time: 50 minutes

Ingredients:

- 1 kilo of beef tenderloin
- 2 shallots
- 1 carrot
- 1 lemon
- 1 orange
- 1 sprig of rosemary
- 400 ml of brandy
- 200 ml of beef broth
- Salt and pepper to taste
- Olive oil to taste

Directions:

1. Peel and wash the shallots and carrots and then chop them. Wash and dry the beef, brush it with olive oil, and sprinkle with salt and pepper. Put the fillet in a roasting pan.
2. Add the carrot and shallots and sprinkle with the brandy.
3. Preheat the Pit Boss at 356 ° F for 15 minutes with the lid closed. Place the roasting pan with the meat on the indirect heat grill. Cook with the lid closed for 25 minutes.
4. Meanwhile, wash the rosemary, chop it, and put it in a bowl.
5. Wash and dry the lemon and orange and grate the peels.
6. Put them in the bowl with the rosemary. Cover with olive oil and mix well.
7. After 25 minutes, open the lid and put the flavored oil over the roast.
8. Close and continue cooking for another 25 minutes.
9. Check the core temperature and if it is 149 ° F, remove it from the Pit Boss; otherwise, proceed until the temperature is reached.
10. As soon as cooked, remove it from the Pit Boss and let the roast rest for 15 minutes.
11. Now cut it into slices, sprinkle with the cooking juices and serve.

Nutritional Value: Calories 309; Fat 16.5g; Carbohydrates 9g; Protein 30.5g

Recipe 63: Broccoli Pesto Spaghetti

Serving Size: 4

Cooking Time: 35 minutes

Ingredients:

- 8 oz. spaghetti
- 1-pound broccoli, cut into florets
- 2 tablespoons olive oil
- 4 garlic cloves, chopped
- 4 basil leaves
- 2 tablespoons blanched almonds
- 1 lemon, juiced
- Salt and pepper to taste

Directions:

1. For the pesto, combine the broccoli, oil, garlic, basil, lemon juice, and almonds in a blender and pulse until well mixed and smooth.
2. Cook the spaghetti in a large pot of salty water for 8 minutes or until al dente. Drain well.
3. Mix the warm spaghetti with the broccoli pesto and serve right away.

Nutritional Value: Calories 284; Fat 10.2g; Carbohydrates 40.2g; Protein 10.4g

Recipe 64: Buttered Rib-Eye Steak

Serving Size: 4

Cooking Time: 50 minutes

Ingredients:

- 1 (24-ounce) bone-in Tomahawk rib-eye, about 2 ½ inches thick
- Olive oil
- Sea salt
- Fresh cracked pepper
- 2 tablespoons premium French butter
- ½ teaspoon Herbes de Provence

Directions:

1. Beat butter with herbs in a small mixing bowl, cover and refrigerate until ready to grill rib-eye.
2. Rub the rib-eye liberally with olive oil, salt and pepper until entire steak is covered.
3. Wrap lightly with cling wrap and place in the refrigerator to marinate for 12 hours.
4. Preheat the griddle to high heat on one side and medium low on the other side, at least one hour prior to cooking.
5. Remove the prepared steak from the refrigerator and leave at room temperature during the hour that the griddle is preheating.
6. Place the prepared steak on the center of the hottest side of the griddle. Do this for both sides, approximately about 10 minutes.
7. Move the rib-eye to the cooler side of the griddle and cook to rare, about 25 to 30 minutes.
8. Transfer rib-eye to a grill rack, add herbed butter on top, and lightly tent it with tin foil to actually rest for at least 15 minutes before carving.
9. Serve with your favorite sides!

Nutritional Value: Calories 273; Fat 2g; Carbohydrates 11g; Protein 9.3g

Recipe 65: Cabbage and Beef Steaks

Serving Size: 4

Cooking Time: 55 minutes

Ingredients:

- 1 lb. chuck steak
- 1 headcanon cabbage, grated
- 1/4 cup olive oil
- 3 tablespoons coconut flour
- 1 teaspoon Italian mixed herb blend
- 1 cup of bone broth

Directions:

1. Preheat the oven to a heat of 380 F. Cut the steak into thin strips across the grain using an abrasive knife. Put in the coconut flour and the steak slices in a zipper bag. Close the bag and shake it to coat. Create little mounds of cabbage in a well-greased baking dish. Serve with olive oil.
2. Then, remove the meat strips made of coconut flour Shake off any excess flour, and place 3-4 beef strips on each cabbage mound. Sprinkle with the Italian herb mix and drizzle it with the olive oil remaining. Roast for about 30 minutes. Take the pan off and add the broth. Place back in the oven and cook for another 10 minutes, or until the meat is cooked. Serve and Enjoy!

Nutritional Value: Calories 331; Fat 20g; Carbohydrates 4.5g; Protein 23g

Recipe 66: Cacciatore Black Olive Chicken

Serving Size: 6

Cooking Time: 15 minutes

Ingredients:

- 6–8 bone-in chicken drumsticks or mixed drumsticks and thighs
- 1 cup chicken stock
- 1 bay leaf
- ½ cup black olives pitted
- 1 medium yellow onion, roughly chopped
- 1 teaspoon dried oregano
- 1 teaspoon garlic powder
- 1 (28-ounce) can stewed tomato puree

Directions:

1. Open the top lid of your Instant Pot.
2. Add the stock, bay leaf, and salt; stir to combine with a wooden spatula.
3. Add the chicken, tomato puree, onion, garlic powder, and oregano; stir again.
4. Close the lid and make sure that the valve is sealed properly.
5. Press MANUAL and set the timer to 15 minutes.
6. The Instant Pot will start building pressure; allow the mixture to cook for the set time.
7. When the timer reads zero, press NPR for natural pressure release. It will take 8–10 minutes to release the pressure.
8. Open the lid and remove the bay leaf.
9. Serve warm with the black olives on top.

Nutritional Value: Calories 309; Fat 16.5g; Carbohydrates 9g; Protein 30.5g

Recipe 67: Coconut Shrimp Stew

Serving Size: 6

Cooking Time: 15 minutes

Ingredients:

- 1 cup coconut milk
- 2 tablespoon lime juice
- ¼ cup diced roasted peppers
- 1 ½ lb. shrimp
- ¼ cup olive oil
- 1 minced garlic clove
- Salt to taste
- 14 oz diced tomatoes
- 2 tablespoon Sriracha sauce
- ¼ cup chopped onions
- ¼ cup chopped cilantro
- Chopped fresh dill for garnish
- Black pepper to taste

Directions:

1. Have the oil in a pot to melt over medium heat.
2. Cook the onions for 3 minutes or until translucent.
3. Mix in the garlic for another minute. Add the peppers, tomatoes, shrimp, and cilantro.
4. Cook until the shrimp becomes opaque for about 3-4 minutes. Stir in the Sriracha sauce and coconut milk and cook for 2 more minutes.
5. Do not bring to a boil.
6. Mix in the salt and lime juice as you stir. Spoon stew in bowls, garnish with the fresh dill and serve warm.

Nutritional Value: Calories 454; Fat 19.2g; Carbohydrates 60.9g; Protein 15g

Recipe 68: Dijon and Herb Pork Tenderloin

Serving Size: 6

Cooking Time: 30 minutes

Ingredients:

- ½ cup fresh Italian parsley leaves
- 3 tablespoons fresh rosemary leaves
- 3 tablespoons fresh thyme leaves
- 3 tablespoons Dijon mustard
- 1 tablespoon extra-virgin olive oil
- 4 garlic cloves, minced
- ½ teaspoon sea salt
- ¼ teaspoon freshly ground black pepper
- 1 (1½-pound) pork tenderloin

Directions:

1. Preheat the oven to 400°F.
2. In a blender, pulse parsley, rosemary, thyme, mustard, olive oil, garlic, sea salt, and pepper. Spread the mixture evenly over the pork and place it on a rimmed baking sheet.
3. Bake for about 20 minutes. Pull out from the oven and put aside for 10 minutes before slicing and serving.

Nutritional Value: Calories 393; Fat 12g; Carbohydrates 74g; Protein 23g

Recipe 69: Fresh Tomato Shrimp Pasta

Serving Size: 4

Cooking Time: 15 minutes

Ingredients:

- 8 ounces whole-wheat spaghetti or linguine
- 2 tablespoons olive oil
- 8 ounces shrimp, raw or precooked, shells and tails removed
- 2 cups diced tomatoes
- 1 cup baby spinach
- ½ teaspoon jarred minced garlic

Directions:

1. Boil the pasta
2. While the pasta is cooking, shimmer the olive oil in a large pan. Cook for 10 minutes until the shrimp are pink and opaque, adding the tomatoes, spinach, and garlic as needed.
3. Toss the pasta with the sauce and shrimp in a large mixing bowl until thoroughly mixed.

Nutritional Value: Calories 331; Fat 20g; Carbohydrates 4.5g; Protein 23g

Recipe 70: Garlic Parmesan Zoodles

Serving Size: 1

Cooking Time: 10 minutes

Ingredients:

- 1 zucchini
- 2 cloves of garlic (diced)
- ¾ tablespoon of olive oil
- 2 teaspoon of parmesan cheese (grated)
- ¼ teaspoon of parsley (dried)
- ¼ teaspoon of paprika
- Parsley (chopped)
- Kosher salt
- Black pepper powder

Directions:

1. Preheat the oven to 400°F.
2. Place foil paper over a baking pan.
3. Cut spirals of zucchini.
4. Take a bowl, add the zoodles, paprika, parsley, garlic, olive oil, salt, and black pepper powder. Mix them well.
5. Place on the baking pan and bake for 10 minutes.
6. Top with parmesan cheese and chopped parsley. Serve hot.

Nutritional Value: Calories 369; Fat 19.9g; Carbohydrates 23.9g; Protein 7.6g

Recipe 71: Ginger and Chili Sea Bass Fillets

Serving Size: 2

Cooking Time: 10 minutes

Ingredients:

- 2 Sea bass fillet
- 1 teaspoon Black pepper
- 1 tablespoon Extra virgin olive oil
- 1 teaspoon Ginger, peeled and chopped
- 1 Garlic cloves, thinly sliced
- 1 red chili, deseeded and thinly sliced
- 2 Green onion stemmed, chopped

Directions:

1. Get a skillet and heat the oil on medium to high heat.
2. Sprinkle black pepper over the Sea Bass and score the fish's skin a few times with a sharp knife.
3. Add the sea bass fillet to the very hot pan with the skin side down.
4. Cook for 5 minutes and turn over.
5. Cook for a further 2 minutes.
6. Remove seabass from the pan and rest.
7. Put the chili, garlic, and ginger and cook for approximately 2 minutes or until golden.
8. Remove from the heat and add the green onions.
9. Scatter the vegetables over your sea bass to serve.
10. Try with a steamed sweet potato or side salad.

Nutritional Value: Calories 454; Fat 19.2g; Carbohydrates 60.9g; Protein 15g

Recipe 72: Herb and Citrus Turkey

Serving Size: 10

Cooking Time: 4 hours

Ingredients:

- whole turkey, neck, and giblets removed
- Zest and juice from 1 lemon
- ½ cup butter
- ½ shallot, chopped
- Sage leaves
- Rosemary, dried
- Thyme, chopped
- 1 garlic clove, minced
- 1 yellow onion, roughly chopped
- Carrots, roughly chopped
- Celery stalks, chopped
- 1 cup dry white wine
- 1 cup chicken stock
- ¼ cup whole wheat flour

Directions:

1. Place lemon zest and juice in a food processor, add butter, shallot, sage, thyme, rosemary, garlic, and pulse. Lift skin from turkey breast without detaching it, rub it with 3 tablespoons of the herb butter under the skin, and secure with toothpicks. Season the cavity and the whole turkey with salt and pepper to taste and place in a baking dish.
2. Add onion, carrots, and celery, tie ends of turkey legs together, rub the turkey with remaining herb butter, add wine and stock to the pan, place in the oven and bake at 425° F for 30 minutes. Reduce heat to 325° F and bake for 2 hours and 30 minutes. Transfer to a platter, pour veggie drippings through a filter, and reserve 2 ½ cups of drippings.
3. Heat a pan with the reserved chilled herb butter over medium heat, add flour, stir well, and cook for 2 minutes. Add reserved pan drippings, bring to a boil, reduce the temperature, and cook for 5 minutes, stirring occasionally.
4. Cut turkey and serve with the gravy you've just prepared.

Nutritional Value: Calories 287; Fat 4g; Carbohydrates 9g; Protein 12g

Recipe 73: Herb Pork Chops

Serving Size: 6

Cooking Time: 10 minutes

Ingredients:

- 6 pork chops

For brine:

- 2 thyme sprigs
- 2 bay leaves
- 1 tablespoon coriander seeds
- 1 tablespoon juniper berries
- 1 tablespoon peppercorns
- 1/2 cup demerara sugar
- Salt

Directions:

1. Add 1-liter water and all brine ingredients into the pot and bring to boil. Remove the medium-sized pot from heat and let it cool brine completely.
2. Add pork chops in brine and let it marinate for 2 hours.
3. Preheat the griddle to high heat.
4. Spray griddle top with cooking spray.
5. Place pork chops on a hot griddle top and cook for 4-5 minutes on each side.
6. Servings and enjoy.

Nutritional Value: Calories 306; Fat 20g; Carbohydrates 12.9g; Protein 18.2g

Recipe 74: Herbed Corn and Cheese Chile Rellenos

Serving Size: 12

Cooking Time: 1 hour

Ingredients:

- 2 lbs. Ripe tomatoes, chopped
- 4 cloves garlic, chopped
- ½ cup sweet onion, chopped
- 1 jalapeno, stemmed, seeded, and chopped
- 8 large green new Mexican or poblano chiles
- 3 ears sweet corn, husked
- ½ teaspoon Dry oregano, Mexican, crumbled
- 1 teaspoon Ground cumin
- 1 teaspoon Mild chile powder
- ⅛ teaspoon Ground cinnamon
- Salt and freshly ground pepper
- 3 cups grated Monterey jack
- ½ cup Mexican crema
- 1 cup queso fresco, crumbled
- Fresh cilantro leaves

Directions:

1. Set the tomatoes, garlic, onion, and jalapeño in a shallow baking dish and place on the griddle to cook until the tomatoes are soft.
2. Place the liquefied tomato mixture in a blender and blend until smooth. Pour the contents into a saucepan. Combine the cumin, oregano, chile powder, cinnamon, and salt and pepper to taste in a medium-sized mixing bowl.
3. Remove the blistered outer skin off the New Mexican chiles with care, being careful not to tear the flesh. Leave the stem ends intact and avoid tearing the flesh.
4. Remove the prepared corn kernels from the cobs and place them in a large mixing dish.
5. Baking time is about approximately 25-30 minutes, or until the mixture is bubbling and the cheese has completely melted. If preferred, garnish with fresh cilantro leaves and a sprinkle of queso fresco before serving. Enjoy!

Nutritional Value: Calories 206; Fat 14g; Carbohydrates 5g; Protein 9g

Recipe 75: Jumbo Scallops with Sprouts and Prosciutto

Serving Size: 4

Cooking Time: 15 minutes

Ingredients:

- 1 lb. sea scallops, patted dry
- 1–1 ½ lb. Brussels sprouts, thinly sliced
- 4 oz. prosciutto, diced
- 3 garlic cloves, crushed
- 1 ½ tablespoon olive oil
- Sea salt, as needed
- Fresh cracked pepper, as needed
- Garlic powder, as needed
- Juice from ½ lemon
- Zest from ½ lemon
- ¼ cup fresh pecorino Romano cheese, grated

Directions:

1. Season the Brussels sprouts with sea salt, fresh cracked pepper, and garlic powder to taste. Pour 1 ½ tablespoon olive oil, then toss until well-coated and let sit for a while.
2. Season the prepared scallops with sea salt and black pepper to taste. Set aside.
3. Warm your gas griddle to medium heat, then sauté the garlic and prosciutto in ½ tablespoon butter for 1 minute. Toss the Brussels sprouts for 5 minutes, stirring to cook evenly.
4. Dissolve 2 tablespoon butter on medium to medium-high heat on the other side of your griddle. Cook the scallops for 3–4 minutes, stirring.
5. Pour the juice of ½ a lemon and 1 tablespoon butter, continue to cook for 3–4 minutes more.
6. Transfer and serve it with the Brussels sprouts-prosciutto mixture and lemon zest with grated pecorino Romano cheese on top. Enjoy!

Nutritional Value: Calories 200; Fat 11g; Carbohydrates 17g; Protein 9g

Recipe 76: Lamb Lasagna

Serving Size: 4

Cooking Time: 3 hours and 40 minutes

Ingredients:

- 1 pound lamb fillets
- 1 tablespoon olive oil
- 1 garlic clove, minced
- 1 rosemary spring, chopped
- 15 ounces tomato passata
- 14 ounces canned béchamel sauce
- 3 tablespoons parmesan, grated
- 8 ounces lasagna sheets, boiled
- 2 tablespoons breadcrumbs
- 2 mozzarella balls, torn
- 1 tablespoons dressed chicory leaves, chopped

Directions:

1. Heat a pot with the oil over medium heat, add the lamb, rosemary and garlic, toss and cook for 6 minutes.
2. Add the passata, bring to a boil, cover the pot with tin foil and bake at 350 degrees F for 3 hours.
3. Cool the mixture down and shred the meat using 2 forks.
4. Spread a layer of the lamb mix on the bottom of a baking dish, add a layer of lasagna sheets, spread a layer of béchamel and sprinkle some of the mozzarella.
5. Continue layering until all ingredients are used up, then top with mozzarella, parmesan, and breadcrumbs. Bake at 375 degrees F for 40 minutes, cool, slice, divide amongst plates, and serve.
6. Enjoy!

Nutritional Value: Calories 287; Fat 4g; Carbohydrates 9g; Protein 12g

Recipe 77: Lamb Shanks with Red Wine

Serving Size: 4

Cooking Time: 5 hours

Ingredients:

- 2 tablespoons olive oil
- 2 tablespoons flour
- 4 lamb shanks, trimmed
- 1 onion, chopped
- 2 garlic cloves, crushed
- 2/3 cup red wine
- 3 cups tomato sauce

Directions:

1. Heat a skillet over high heat. Add the olive oil.
2. Season the lamb shanks, then roll in the flour. Shake off excess flour and place the shanks in the skillet to brown on all sides.
3. Spray the slow cooker with olive oil and place the browned shanks in the slow cooker.
4. Add the crushed garlic to the red wine. Mix with the tomato sauce and then pour the mixture over the lamb shanks and cook on low for 5–6 hours

Nutritional Value: Calories 354; Fat 12g; Carbohydrates 43g; Protein 16g

Recipe 78: Meatless Spinach Lasagna

Serving Size: 12

Cooking Time: 1 hour and 5 minutes

Ingredients:

- 1/3 cup butter, cubed
- 1/3 cup all-purpose flour
- 3-3/4 cups half-and-half cream
- 1 cup heavy whipping cream
- 3/4 cup grated Parmesan cheese, divided
- 2 cartons (15 oz. each) ricotta cheese
- 1 package (10 oz.) frozen chopped spinach, thawed and squeezed dry
- 3/4 cup shredded carrot
- 12 no-cook lasagna noodles
- 2 cups shredded part-skim mozzarella cheese
- 1/2 cup seasoned bread crumbs
- 1 tablespoon butter, melted

Directions:

1. Melt butter in a big pot; mix in flour until it is smooth. Slowly pour in creams then boil. Cook and mix for 2 mins until the mixture is thick. Mix in half cup Parmesan cheese.
2. Mix remaining Parmesan cheese, ricotta cheese, carrot, and spinach together in a big bowl.
3. In a 13-inch by 9-inch greased baking dish, pour in 3/4 cup sauce mixture then add 4 noodles on top. Let the noodles overlap a little. Spread 1/2 of the ricotta mixture, a cup of sauce, and 2/3 cup of mozzarella. Repeat process. Layer left noodles, sauce, and mozzarella. Mix butter and breadcrumbs; spread the mixture on top of the lasagna until full.
4. Bake in a 375 degrees F oven, covered, for 55 mins. Remove cover and bake for another 10-15 mins until the dish is bubbly. Set aside for 15 mins then cut.

Nutritional Value: Calories 331; Fat 20g; Carbohydrates 4.5g; Protein 23g

Recipe 79: Mussels Curry with Lime

Serving Size: 4

Cooking Time: 10 minutes

Ingredients:

- 2 and ½ pounds mussels, scrubbed
- 14 ounces canned coconut milk
- 3 tablespoons red curry paste
- 1 tablespoon olive oil
- Black pepper to the taste
- ½ cup low-sodium chicken stock
- Juice of 1 lime
- Zest of 1 lime, grated
- ¼ cup cilantro, chopped
- 3 tablespoons basil, chopped

Directions:

1. Heat up a pan with the oil over medium-high heat, add curry paste, stir and cook for 2 minutes.
2. Add stock, black pepper, coconut milk, lime juice, lime zest and mussels, toss, cover the pan and cook for 10 minutes.
3. Divide this into bowls, sprinkle cilantro and basil on top and serve.
4. Enjoy!

Nutritional Value: Calories 260; Fat 12g; Carbohydrates 10g; Protein 12g

Recipe 80: Pan-Roasted Chicken with Carrots

Serving Size: 4

Cooking Time: 40 minutes

Ingredients:

- 4 chicken thighs
- 1 large onion
- 1½ pounds carrots
- A head of garlic
- 4 tablespoon olive oil
- 1 tablespoon fresh rosemary
- Freshly ground black pepper and kosher salt, to taste

Directions:

1. Oil and heat the pan and add the carrots and onions.
2. Remove the top from the garlic; discard place the remaining on the tray.
3. Drizzle the vegetables with approximately 2 tablespoons of olive oil and then season with pepper, rosemary, and salt.
4. Place the chicken thighs on top. Rub the chicken thighs with 1 teaspoon of olive oil and season with pepper and salt.
5. Roast in the preheated oven for 15 to 20 minutes, until the carrots are fork-tender the skin of the chicken turns golden.
6. Evenly divide the cooked chicken thighs and vegetables among four plates. Serve immediately and enjoy.

Nutritional Value: Calories 309; Fat 16.5g; Carbohydrates 9g; Protein 30.5g

Recipe 81: Ravioli with Artichokes and Olives

Serving Size: 4

Cooking Time: 10 minutes

Ingredients:

- 16oz/453g frozen spinach and ricotta ravioli
- 10oz/283g frozen quartered artichoke hearts thawed
- ½ cup oil-packed sun-dried tomatoes
- 15oz/425g no-salt cannellini beans
- 3 tablespoon toasted pine nuts
- ¼ cup Kalamata olives
- ¼ cup chopped fresh basil
- 2 tablespoon olive oil

Directions:

1. In a large pot on heat, cook the ravioli according to package directions. Drain and toss with 1 tablespoon of oil, then set aside.
2. In a nonstick skillet, heat rest oil over medium heat. Add artichokes and beans and sauté for 2 to 3 minutes or till heated thoroughly.
3. Mix the cooked ravioli with sun-dried tomatoes, pine nuts, olives, and basil.

Nutritional Value: Calories 454; Fat 19.2g; Carbohydrates 60.9g; Protein 15g

Recipe 82: Roasted Pesto Trout

Serving Size: 4

Cooking Time: 20 minutes

Ingredients:

- 2 cups chopped fresh basil or 1 cup dried basil
- ½ cup olive oil
- 2 tablespoons pine nuts
- 2 teaspoons jarred minced garlic
- 2 whole trout or 4 trout fillets

Directions:

1. In a bowl, combine the basil, olive oil, pine nuts, and garlic. Choose one of the following methods to make your pesto:
   a) On a large cutting board, use a rolling pin to repeatedly roll-over the mixture, crushing it into a thick paste.
   b) Pulse together in a blender to create a thick paste.
2. If using the whole trout, stuff each trout with half of the pesto.
3. Bake the trout for 15 to 20 minutes until the fish is opaque and flakes easily with a fork.

Nutritional Value: Calories 454; Fat 19.2g; Carbohydrates 60.9g; Protein 15g

Recipe 83: Sriracha Duck Poppers

Serving Size: 1

Cooking Time: 4 hours

Ingredients:

- 8 – 10 pieces of bacon, cut event into same-sized pieces measuring 4 inches each
- 3 duck breasts; boneless and with skin removed and sliced into strips measuring ½ inches
- Sriracha sauce
- 6 de-seeded jalapenos, with the top cut off and sliced into strips

Directions:

6. Wrap the bacon around one trip of pepper and one slice of duck
7. Secure it firmly with the help of a toothpick
8. Fire the griddle on low flame and keep this wrap and griddle it for half an hour until the bacon turns crisp
9. Rotate often to ensure even cooking
10. Serve with sriracha sauce.

Nutritional Value: Calories 291; Fat 19g; Carbohydrates 39g; Protein 29g

Recipe 84: Stovetop Clambake

Serving Size: 4

Cooking Time: 45 minutes

Ingredients:

- 1 lb. small red-skinned potatoes
- 2 whole live lobsters, (about 1½ lbs. each)
- 12 cherrystone, steamer or littleneck clams, scrubbed
- ½ lb. mussels, scrubbed and debearded if necessary
- 4 ears corn, husked and cut into thirds

Directions:

1. In a big stockpot, place in a steamer basket and add 1 inch of water to boil on high heat. Place the potatoes into the basket and steam while covered for 4 minutes. Lower the heat slightly to prevent it from boiling over, if needed.
2. Place the lobsters on top of potatoes, and steam while covered for 4 minutes. Place mussels and clams on top of them then continue to steam, covered, for another 4 minutes. Place the corn on top of everything and cover, then continue to steam for another 4 - 8 minutes until the clams are open and the potatoes are soft.
3. Arrange the potatoes, clams, mussels, and corn onto serving platters. Remove the lobster tails and claws by twisting them away from its body, then cut tails lengthwise and discard bodies. Add the claws and split tails into the platters. Serve right away.

Nutritional Value: Calories 229; Fat 19.9g; Carbohydrates 23.9g; Protein 7.6g

Recipe 85: Texas-Style Rubbed Brisket

Serving Size: 6

Cooking Time: 6 hours 20 minutes

Ingredients:

- 1 (4 ½ lb) flat cut beef brisket (3 inches thick)

For the rub:

- 1 tablespoon sea salt
- 1 tablespoon dark brown sugar
- 2 teaspoons smoked paprika
- 2 teaspoons chili powder
- 1 teaspoon garlic powder
- 1 teaspoon onion powder
- 1 teaspoon ground black pepper
- 1 teaspoon mesquite liquid smoke, like Colgin

Directions:

1. Combine the prepared rub ingredients in a small mixing bowl.
2. Rinse and pat brisket dry and rub with coffee mix.
3. Preheat the griddle for two zone cooking; heat one side to high and leaving one side with low heat.
4. Sear on high heat side for 3 - 5 minutes on each side or until nicely charred.
5. Move to low heat side, tent with foil, and cook for 6 hours or until a meat thermometer registers 195°F.
6. Remove from griddle. Let stand, covered, 30 minutes.
7. Cut the prepared brisket across grain into thin slices and serve.

Nutritional Value: Calories 331; Fat 20g; Carbohydrates 4.5g; Protein 23g

Recipe 86: Tofu in Purgatory

Serving Size: 2

Cooking Time: 25 minutes

Ingredients:

- 4 cloves of garlic, large
- 1 block of un-pressed medium tofu; cut into rounds
- 1 tablespoon olive oil
- 2 teaspoons dried herbs
- Pepper salt to taste
- 1 can diced tomatoes
- ½ teaspoon dried chili flakes
- Indian black salt, optional

Directions:

1. Oil and heat the pan, add cook the garlic until it turns a little brown for a couple of minutes. Add the salt, chili flakes, pepper, and tomatoes herbs.
2. Let simmer for a couple of minutes and then, add the tofu rounds.
3. Decrease the heat to medium-low let simmer until the tofu is soft heated through the sauce thickens, for 12 to 15 minutes.
4. Just before serving, sprinkle your recipe with a small amount of optional Indian black salt.
5. Serve with toast, baguette, or even crusty bread. Enjoy.

Nutritional Value: Calories 309; Fat 16.5g; Carbohydrates 9g; Protein 30.5g

Recipe 87: Tuna with Lemon Butter Sauce

Serving Size: 4

Cooking Time: 5 minutes

Ingredients:

- 4 tuna fillets
- 1/4 cup lemon juice
- 1 tablespoon fresh dill
- 1 tablespoon butter

Directions:

1. Pour 1 cup water and lemon juice into the Instant Pot.
2. Add the steamer basket.
3. Put the tuna fillet on top of the basket.
4. Season with salt and pepper and dill.
5. Seal the pot.
6. Choose the manual setting.
7. Cook at high pressure for 5 minutes.
8. Release the pressure quickly.
9. Remove from the pot.
10. Place the butter on top.
11. Let it melt, and then serve.

Nutritional Value: Calories 213; Fat 18.5g; Carbohydrates 1g; Protein 10.8g

Recipe 88: Turkey Tenderloin with Lemon-Dijon Artichoke

Serving Size: 2

Cooking time: 15 minutes

Ingredients

- 8 ounces turkey tenderloin, cut into 1-inch pieces
- 1 teaspoon sea salt, plus more to taste
- 1½ teaspoons freshly ground black pepper, plus more to taste
- 1 tablespoon avocado oil or extra-virgin olive oil
- ½ red bell pepper, diced
- ¼ cup low-carb dry white wine or chicken broth
- 4 garlic cloves, chopped
- ¼ cup roughly chopped canned or thawed frozen artichoke hearts
- ¼ cup heavy (whipping) cream
- 1 tablespoon Dijon mustard
- ½ tablespoon fresh thyme leaves
- Juice of ½ lemon
- 2 tablespoons chopped fresh parsley

Directions

1. Season the turkey with salt and black pepper.
2. Heat the oil, then cook the turkey for 3 minutes on each side. Add the bell pepper and cook for 1 minute, or until it starts to soften.
3. Reduce the heat to medium-low and add the wine and garlic. Using a wooden spoon or spatula, scrape up all the bits on the bottom of the pan. Add the artichoke hearts, cream, mustard, and thyme. Simmer for 5 to 7 minutes, stirring, until the sauce starts to thicken. Add the lemon juice and season with more salt and black pepper.
4. Divide the turkey and vegetables between two plates. Garnish with parsley and serve.

Nutritional Value: Calories 287; Fat 4g; Carbohydrates 9g; Protein 12g

Recipe 89: Turkey with Cream-Cheese Sauce

Serving Size: 4

Cooking Time: 20 minutes

Ingredients:

- 2 cups heavy whipping cream
- 7 oz. cream cheese
- 1 tablespoon tamari soy sauce
- 2 tablespoon butter
- 1½ pounds turkey breast
- Pepper salt to taste
- 1½ oz. small capers

Directions:

1. Oil and heat the pan. Generously season the turkey with pepper salt; carefully fry until it turns golden brown all around.
2. Finish cooking the meat in the preheated oven. When done, place the cooked turkey on a clean, large plate; tent with aluminum foil.
3. Pour the turkey drippings into a small-sized saucepan. Add cream cheese and cream. Give the ingredients a good stir bring to a light boil. Once done, decrease the heat let simmer for a couple of minutes until thickened. Add the soy sauce, season with pepper and salt.
4. Serve the turkey with fried capers and sauce. Enjoy.

Nutritional Value: Calories 301; Fat 11g; Carbohydrates 23g; Protein 6.7g

Recipe 90: Warm Salmon and Brussels Sprouts

Serving Size: 4

Cooking Time: 10 minutes

Ingredients:

- 4 (4-ounce) salmon fillets, skinless
- 1 pound Brussels sprouts, shredded or chopped
- 1 cup fresh cranberries
- 8 ounces endive, chopped
- 1 lemon, halved
- 2 tablespoons olive oil, divided
- ¼ cup unsalted pecan pieces

Directions:

1. Heat 1 tablespoon of olive oil on medium heat in a medium sauté pan or skillet until shimmering.
2. Simultaneously, in a large sauté pan or skillet, heat the remaining 1 tablespoon of olive oil on medium heat.
3. Pat your salmon fillets dry using paper towels. In the first (medium) pan, sear the salmon on one side and cook for 5 minutes.
4. Flip, then sear the other side and cook for 5 additional minutes. The fish should be opaque and flake easily with a fork.
5. In the second (large) pan, sauté the Brussels sprouts, cranberries, and endive for 10 minutes, stirring frequently.
6. Serve the salmon over the vegetables and cranberries, with a squeeze of fresh lemon juice and pecan pieces on top.

Nutritional Value: Calories 309; Fat 16.5g; Carbohydrates 9g; Protein 30.5g

Chapter 5: Dessert Recipes

Recipe 91: Banana Walnut Bread

Serving Size: 10

Cooking Time: 1 hour and 20 minutes

Ingredients:

- 3 bananas, medium
- ½ cup walnuts
- 3 eggs, large
- 1 teaspoon baking soda
- 2 cups almond flour
- ¼ cup olive oil
- Coconut oil

Directions:

1. Oil the pan and heat it.
2. Cut up the bananas and then add the real ingredients in a large-sized mixing bowl; mix until combined well.
3. Pour the mixture into the prepared loaf pan and bake for 55 to 60 minutes.

Nutritional Value: Calories 213; Fat 1.4g; Carbohydrates 23.9g; Protein 1.9g

Recipe 92: Brown Rice Pudding

Serving Size: 4

Cooking Time: 55 minutes

Ingredients:

- 1 cup brown rice, uncooked
- 1 teaspoon vanilla
- ½ teaspoon cinnamon
- 6-8 drops liquid stevia
- 1 cup skim milk
- 1 mango, peeled and sliced
- 2 cups water
- 1/8 teaspoon salt

Directions:

1. Add water and salt to a large saucepan and bring to boil.
2. Add rice and stir well.
3. Reduce heat and simmer within 35-40 minutes or until rice is tender.
4. Mash mango slices with a fork. Stir mashed mango, cinnamon, stevia, and milk into the rice.
5. Cook over low heat for 10-15 minutes more or until liquid is absorbed.
6. Remove pan from heat. Add vanilla and stir well.
7. Serve and enjoy.

Nutritional Value: Calories 117; Fat 9g; Carbohydrates 7g; Protein 1g

Recipe 93: Butter Walnut and Raisin Cookies

Serving Size: 8

Cooking Time: 15 minutes

Ingredients:

- ½ teaspoon pure almond extract
- ½ teaspoon pure vanilla extract
- 2 tablespoons rum
- ½ cup almond flour
- 1 stick butter, room temperature
- 1/3 cup cornflour
- 2 tablespoons Truvia
- ¼ cup raisins
- 1/3 cup walnuts, ground

Directions:

1. In a small bowl, place rum and raisins and allow to sit for 15-minutes. Beat the butter with Truvia, vanilla, and almond extract until light and fluffy in a mixing dish. Then, throw in both types of flour and ground almonds. Fold in the soaked raisins.
2. Continue mixing until it forms a dough. Refrigerate for approximately 20 minutes after covering. Meanwhile, preheat the air-fryer to 330°Fahrenheit. Roll the dough into small cookies, place them in an air-fryer cake pan; gently press each cookie with a spoon. Bake cookies for 15-minutes.

Nutritional Value: Calories 406; Fat 11.3g; Carbohydrates 62.3g; Protein 5.7g

Recipe 94: Chia Sesame Balls

Serving Size: 2

Cooking Time: 4 minutes

Ingredients:

- 1 tablespoon rice malt syrup
- 2 tablespoon sesame seeds, toasted
- 1/3 c. toasted macadamias
- 1 c. pitted dried dates
- 1/3 cup dry roasted cashews
- 2 tablespoon white chia seeds

Directions:

1. Place half of the sesame seeds, macadamia, cashews, chia seeds, dates, and rice malt syrup in a blender or food processor.
2. Pulse the ingredients until a well-mixed, paste-like, thick, and smooth mixture is formed.
3. Transfer the mixture into a shallow dish.
4. Place the remaining sesame seeds on a plate. Scoop out 2 tablespoons of the nut-seeds mixture. Roll into balls.
5. Coat the balls by rolling on the sesame seeds.
6. Place the coated balls on a plate.
7. Chill to set the balls in the refrigerator.
8. Serve once firm.

Nutritional Value: Calories 238; Fat 2g; Carbohydrates 19g; Protein 5g

Recipe 95: Cinnamon Stuffed Peaches

Serving Size: 4

Cooking Time: 15 minutes

Ingredients:

- 4 peaches, pitted, halved
- 2 tablespoons ricotta cheese
- 2 tablespoons of liquid honey
- ¾ cup of water
- ½ teaspoon vanilla extract
- ¾ teaspoon ground cinnamon
- 1 tablespoon of almonds, sliced
- ¾ teaspoon saffron

Directions:

1. Pour water in the saucepan and bring to boil.
2. Add vanilla extract, saffron, ground cinnamon, and liquid honey.
3. Cook the liquid until the honey is melted.
4. Then remove it from the heat.
5. Put the halved peaches in the hot honey liquid.
6. Meanwhile, make the filling: mix up together ricotta cheese, vanilla extract, and sliced almonds.
7. Remove the peaches from the honey liquid and arrange them on the plate. Fill 4 peach halves with ricotta filling and cover them with remaining peach halves.
8. Sprinkle the cooked dessert with liquid honey mixture gently.

Nutritional Value: Calories 213; Fat 1.4g; Carbohydrates 23.9g; Protein 1.9g

Recipe 96: Ginger Date Bars

Serving Size: 8

Cooking Time: 20 minutes

Ingredients:

- ¾ cup dates pitted
- 1 ½ cups almond, soaked in overnight water
- ¼ cup almond milk
- 1 teaspoon ginger, grounded

Directions:

1. Preheat your oven to 350 degrees F.
2. Place the almond in a food processor.
3. Pulse it until you get a thick dough form.
4. Press the dough in a baking dish lined with parchment paper.
5. Set it aside.
6. Make a date mix by combining the rest of the ingredients in your food processor.
7. Pour the date mixture onto the almond crust.
8. Bake for 20 minutes.
9. Allow it to cool before you slice them.
10. Serve and enjoy!

Nutritional Value: Calories 309; Fat 16.5g; Carbohydrates 9g; Protein 30.5g

Recipe 97: Honey Sesame Cookies

Serving Size: 2

Cooking Time: 15 minutes

Ingredients:

- 3 cups flour
- 1 cup sugar
- 1 cup butter
- 2 eggs
- 3 tablespoon honey
- 1 cup pistachio nuts, roughly chopped
- 1 cup sesame seeds
- 1 tablespoon vinegar
- 1 teaspoon vanilla
- 1 teaspoon baking powder
- a pinch of salt

Directions:

1. Scourge the butter and the sugar until light and fluffy. Gently add in the eggs, then the vanilla extract, and the vinegar. In a large mixing basin, whisk together the flour, salt, and baking powder. Beat until just incorporated. Cover and refrigerate for an hour.
2. Mix the sesame seeds and the honey on a medium plate. Place the pistachios in another one. Take a teaspoonful of dough, form it into a ball, then dip it into the pistachios. Press a little and dip it into the sesame-honey mixture. Repeat with the remaining dough, arranging the cookies on a lined baking sheet.
3. Bake the cookies in a preheated to 350 F oven for 15 minutes, or until they turn light brown. Set aside in the baking sheet for 2-3 minutes, then move to a wire rack.

Nutritional Value: Calories 117; Fat 9g; Carbohydrates 7g; Protein 1g

Recipe 98: Peanut Butter Cookies

Serving Size: 2

Cooking Time: 15 minutes

Ingredients:

- 1 teaspoon vanilla extract
- 1 cup whole wheat flour
- ¼ teaspoon salt
- ½ cup honey
- ⅓ cup plain unsweetened non-dairy milk
- 1 teaspoon baking soda
- 1 cup creamy peanut butter

Directions:

1. In a large basin, mix the flour, baking soda, and salt. In a second dish, mix the peanut butter, honey, nondairy milk, and vanilla.
2. Combine the wet and dry components with clean or gloved hands. The dough will be too stiff to mix with a spoon. Knead the dough until there are no patches of dry ingredients remaining.
3. Make 24 balls, each with 1 heaping tablespoon of dough. Place each ball at least 1 inch apart on the prepared baking sheets. Using the back of a fork, flatten each cookie in a crisscross pattern.
4. Bake the cookies for 10 minutes for a chewy texture or 12 to 13 minutes for crispier cookies.
5. Serve warm or cooled.

Nutritional Value: Calories 217; Fat 9g; Carbohydrates 7g; Protein 1g

Recipe 99: Pistachio Rice Pudding

Serving Size: 2

Cooking Time: 5 minutes

Ingredients:

- 1 cup cooked brown rice
- 2 tablespoon pistachios, chopped
- ½ teaspoon tapioca starch
- ¼ teaspoon vanilla
- ¼ teaspoon cinnamon
- 1 cup unsweetened almond milk
- 1 tablespoon honey

Directions:

1. Add rice, vanilla, cinnamon, honey, and almond milk in a small saucepan and stir well.
2. Bring the rice mixture to a boil.
3. Turn heat to medium and simmer until all liquid is absorbed.
4. Remove saucepan from heat.
5. Add pistachios and tapioca starch and stir for a minute.
6. Serve and enjoy.

Nutritional Value: Calories 217; Fat 9g; Carbohydrates 7g; Protein 1g

Recipe 100: Wrapped Plums

Serving Size: 8

Cooking Time: 0 minutes

Ingredients:

- 2 oz prosciutto, cut into 16 pieces
- 4 plums, quartered
- 1 tablespoon chives, chopped
- A pinch of red pepper flakes, crushed

Directions:

1. Wrap each of your plum quarters with a prosciutto slice,
2. Put them all on a platter, sprinkle the chives plus pepper flakes all over, and serve.

Nutritional Value: Calories 213; Fat 1.4g; Carbohydrates 23.9g; Protein 1.9g

• Conclusion

Refined carbohydrates, candy, and sweets all include glucose, which is easily broken down. As a result, after eating these items, blood glucose levels rise quickly. Blood sugars rise steadily and slowly after eating more complex, unprocessed carbs (oatmeal, apples, baked potatoes, etc.) that require more digestive stages before glucose can be produced. When blood glucose levels rise rapidly, the body must react swiftly by releasing huge amounts of insulin all at once, or risk developing hyperglycemia, a severe condition (high blood sugar). alpha-insulin

While glucose levels change rapidly, insulin levels change considerably more slowly. The bloodstream becomes swiftly overwhelmed with glucose when a lot of simple sugar is consumed. In response to the increased sugar, the pancreas releases insulin. While glucose enters cells quickly, high insulin levels result in an excess of insulin in the blood, which can cause starvation and even serious hypoglycemia (low blood sugar). There is actually less of a need for drastic correction as blood glucose levels rise consistently.

This more gradual phase can make you feel "complete" or "satisfied" for a longer period of time. For these reasons, it is important to actually limit the amount and frequency of sweets and refined sugars in your diet for overall health. Instead, eat more complex sugars such as fresh bananas, whole wheat bread and pasta, and beans. The gap between simple and complex sugars is exemplified by the contrast between white (basic) and whole wheat (more complex) bread (carbohydrates).

Insulin is required for a cell to utilize glucose. Insulin production or cell understanding issues can easily throw the body's carefully regulated glucose metabolism mechanism out of whack. When one of these problems happens, blood sugar levels rise and decrease and the body is at danger of contracting diabetes.

Diabetes is a blood sugar (glucose) and insulin-related disease in which a person's capacity to create and use insulin, a pancreatic hormone that lowers blood sugar levels by transferring it from the bloodstream to the body's cells, is impaired.

Type 1 diabetes actually develops when the pancreas is damaged or fails to generate insulin owing to autoimmune or other unique causes. Although it is actually most commonly diagnosed in children, this kind of diabetes can also affect adults.

In type 2 diabetes, both the pancreas production of insulin (insulin insufficiency) and the body's use of insulin are impaired (insulin resistance). Blood sugar levels rise as the pancreas loses its ability to generate enough insulin to overcome the body's resistance to it. Blood arteries can be damaged by too much glucose in the blood, which is a problem.

Furthermore, the body's tissues are unable to utilize glucose properly for energy when it remains in the bloodstream rather than entering the cells.

It's important to remember that high blood sugar levels are the result of an underlying mechanism that has been operating for years until blood sugar levels reach dangerously high levels.

Finally, diabetes is not a death sentence. With prayers and a good eating habit, you can counter diabetes thereby maintaining a total body healing.

Manufactured by Amazon.ca
Bolton, ON

32795345R00061